Short Stories
and
Small Miracles

By Jeane Schwarzkopf

iii

Many thanks to....

Pauline Nevins, who encouraged me to record my stories
and transcribed them into short-story form

Jan Tannarome, who took the short stories and made the first draft of a book

Cynthia Hoven, who edited the texts and brought this book into its present form

Arline Williams, who is no longer here on Earth, but who was a writer and editor
and the first person to approach me about writing down some of my stories.

iv

Words of Gratitude

I write in gratitude and thanks to many whom I've met in my life. Some I've described here at length, some appear only briefly, and others have not found their way into these pages. I want to especially give thanks here to:

* _my parents, who gave me a place to plant the seed of incarnation_
* _my sisters and entire family for all their love_
* _my first husband, Harry, for mentioning that he had gone to a talk by an East Indian teacher who spoke about the "I AM" as we drove down Sunset Boulevard, for these words "I AM" had a great impact on me when I heard them for the first time_
* _my dear Friedemann, who showed me a very cultivated, articulate and exciting world, a European world filled with real intelligence and sophistication, and carried within himself a great and warm heart, the mind of a scholar, and the will of a lion_
* _George, my dear partner, who has been a wonderful companion since Friedemann's death_
* _Dr. Alberto Villoldo, a friend and teacher who showed me the way of the shaman and provided tools for life, tools that allowed for healing others as well as myself_
* _Rudolf Steiner, whose works and teachings gave me an ability to find word form to describe the spiritual, conceptual world. His works touched all areas of my life, for after studying eurythmy for six years in Switzerland, I went on to teach, perform and to heal many people who entered my life._

All my various studies led me to a life of movement and healing. Now, at the age of 77, I continue to do all I can, wherever I am, to serve all I meet.

None of us know how long we will live, but whether my life continues for another day or another twenty years, I can say in truth for myself that my life has been one great experience, for which I am deeply grateful. On rare occasions the veil has lifted and I have glimpsed another knowing, another realizing. If even for a few moments, I have found myself sitting under the Bodhi Tree.

PART ONE

CHILDHOOD

Death is so final.

In 1947, a young drunk driver, running a red light, hit my father's car. My father was in a coma for three days and then passed on, leaving me and this world behind. I was nine years old.

Our mother did not allow my sisters or me to attend the funeral. She wanted us to keep a living memory of him, and not think of him as dead. She did this to protect us, but, in my case, it prevented me from being able to create closure of that chapter of my life. For the next five years, I continued to believe that my father would come walking through the door one day.

My father was the only external authority I had ever truly recognized or respected, and I adored him. His presence was so strong and assuring that after his death I actually felt physically lopsided and less whole, as if some part of me was missing. With the vulnerable thoughts of a child, I thought that my schoolmates could see that he was gone simply by looking at me and seeing me lean to one side or the other.

My father was not a religious man. He did, however, have deep spiritual principles which he lived by and passed on to us. One of these was: "NO ONE IS ABOVE OR BELOW YOU." The other was, "YOUR WORD IS YOUR BEING." These two principles were very important to me throughout my life. Even in my early years, I sometimes found myself deeply disappointed with many people who did not keep their word. It took me a good part of my life to develop the compassion for others necessary to overcome this disappointment.

1

Looking back, I see how my father's death was the beginning of my liberation, because he was the one sole authority I ever accepted in my life. From that point on, I listened with openness to all people, but deeply knew that I was the one who would determine what the truth was for me. This authority figure had given me so much that there was never again someone who could scale those heights.

Exactly one week before my father's death, a sudden heart attack had claimed my mother's much younger brother. My grandparents and extended family went to New York from California to attend his funeral, but my mother chose to remain in California with my father, me and my two sisters, for it would have been too difficult for her to travel alone with the three of us.

Thus it was that she was alone when my father died. At the time of his death, he was 36 and she only 35. They had just moved to California and were beginning to build their new life there. My father's death devastated my mother, and she never fully recovered from it. She was still in shock over her brother's death one week earlier, and now found herself alone, in California, with her three young daughters, ages thirteen, nine and three years old.

Sometimes I heard my mother crying alone in her room at night, and I remember thinking, "If only I could make her happy! If only I could help her stop crying..." But no matter how much I wished this for her, it was not mine to do for her, and she continued to struggle. In her despair, she started drinking. At first she drank only a little, but over time she began to drink more and more. Through it all, however, she was a strong and determined woman, and her powerful will got me and my sisters through to adulthood.

....

My parents first met at a dance hall in New York in the 1920's. They both loved ballroom dancing, and they were a handsome couple. She was slender and beautiful with olive skin and dark hair, and he was strong and healthy with clear hazel eyes, fair skin and light brown hair.

2

After they married, they made their first home in Brooklyn in a small brownstone house. There my two sisters and I were born and spent our earliest years.

One early childhood memory from our life in Brooklyn is vivid. I was already walking, so I could have been one and a half years old, but not older than two. I remember crawling around in the vegetable beds of my mother's garden, trying to be as close to the earth as possible. I loved its rich smell, especially when it was moist, and I wanted to taste it. Mom would scold me for eating "dirt" and tell me not to do it anymore. To me, however, it was Earth, and I loved it. I had to find a way to keep eating it. Even at that young age, I planned how to eat it so carefully that my mother wouldn't notice. I believed that if I didn't get any of it on the outside of my mouth, she would never know. But the minute I walked into the house, she scolded me again!

"How does she know?" I thought, as she scolded me time and time again. It seemed to me that mothers were miraculous, psychic beings who always were aware of what their children were doing! Of course, I probably had a mineral deficiency and she could see dirt in my teeth, but there was a magic surrounding those moments that has stayed alive in my memory. I was astounded that she always knew what I had done. To me, it seemed that mothers knew *everything!*

My father had a very powerful presence. All he ever had to do was look at us when we were not behaving and we corrected ourselves. He always asked us to go to our rooms until we were once again in harmony, so we had to work out any discords ourselves. This empowered us to take responsibilities for our actions, for the rest of our lives.

Our childhood friends were likewise impressed by my father. Whenever he walked into a room, we all shaped up immediately. Yet even with his strong, grounded presence, my father enjoyed life and laughter. He had a wonderful gramophone, and our home was always filled with the music he loved, including jazz, the pop music of the day, and the classics.

When I was six years old, we moved from Brooklyn to California. Among other things, the journey marked the beginning of my powerful relationship to spirituality. There were six of us in the car: my mom, my aunt and uncle, my two sisters and me. One afternoon as we were driving through Arizona, my family stopped the car and got out to take a short walk, leaving me asleep in the back seat. Suddenly I woke out of a deep sleep, sat up, and looked out. I was completely alone, in the car, in the desert. In that quiet space, I was awestruck. It felt to me as if paint had been poured down from heaven all over the landscape. Shortly afterwards, my family returned and we all walked together. But that first perception that I had, all by myself with the Painted Desert, began my relationship with the desert as an integral part of my spiritual destiny.

....

In 1945, Southern California was still very pure and very beautiful---- God's Land. My father moved there to set up a business and buy us a beautiful house, our dream home.

At that time, preschools and kindergartens did not exist. We started school when we were seven and ready for first grade. My older sister and I spent our free time playing outside since there was no television at that time. We loved gymnastics and making up our own routines. It was nothing for my sister to balance me up on her hands while I was in a handstand.

We also loved all forms of dance. Our California house had a large front room, and there was a thick brown sheepskin rug in front of the fireplace. My father played music on the gramophone and encouraged me to dance. He would say, "Jeane, now you are in the storm and wind." He helped stir my imagination, telling me only to express myself however I wanted. I danced in total improvisation, with movements that resembled an Isadora Duncan dance.

Here, already in my early years, were two themes that became seeds for my growth: music and dance. Through my early exposure to music through my father, I awakened to a true love for classical music. It was such a strong feeling I can honestly say I believe it was a re- awakening. He introduced me to Claude Debussy's *Claire de Lune*, which touched me so deeply that it helped me shape my lifelong goal of becoming a dancer. For many years after my father's death, however, I cried whenever I heard this piece because I missed him so much.

All of our relatives followed in my father's footsteps, and within five years of our transition to the West Coast, most of my mother's family moved out to California. Thus it was that, despite the loss of my father, we were surrounded by the care and love of grandparents, aunts, uncles and cousins. Because of my father's death, my mother sold our family home and went back to work. We moved into an apartment adjacent to our grandparents' house. There was a big door between our apartment and their kitchen so we could go from kitchen to kitchen, and we lived as one big family.

Money was not easy to come by in those years. My grandparents cared for us while my mom worked as a seamstress at a Levi Strauss jeans factory in downtown Los Angeles. I am deeply grateful for her dedication to us, and for how had she worked all those years to bring us through life honorably, even with the minimal educational skills typical of women in the late 1940's and '50's.

Years later, when we were settled in Hollywood, I was able to get a job working at the phone company. Soon afterwards, I was able to help my mother get a job there also. This was a much better situation for her.

. . . .

The Italian side of my family was Roman Catholic. My father had been Greek Orthodox, but he was not religious in any traditional way, and he was content to allow our mom make decisions about our religious upbringing. Every Sunday we attended mass together in our neighborhood church, which was big and very beautiful.

When I was eleven, I walked to church one Saturday afternoon to go to confession. Kneeling inside the confessional, I revealed to the priest that a boy had kissed me and touched my breast. I was already embarrassed at having to expose myself like that, but I became mortified as the priest continued to question me about my experience. He gave me penance, and I left the dark confessional feeling really, really awful.

I was still standing just outside the confessional when I had a very strange feeling. I slowly turned around, and saw that the confessional curtain had been pushed slightly aside and the priest was peeping out at me. He had interrogated me and then he had to satisfy his curiosity about who I was.

This was the awakening of my realization that I could trust my own intuitions. I had first sensed this "invasion" and then I saw it. I immediately walked up to the statue of the Sacred Heart of Christ, his arms held open. I said to him, "I believe in you, but I do not believe in this way," and I walked out of that church. That ended my connection to "church."

....

When I was fourteen, my mother and grandparents saw that our neighborhood in Los Angeles was becoming a bit rough. They decided it was time to move on, and we all moved to Hollywood.

In many ways, our family was a typical 1950's family. The grown-ups were simple people, with very little education or sophistication. Our lifestyle was colored by their rich Italian heritage and its strong family values. In their yards, they grew some of their own food, along with lots of flowers. Holiday festivals were grand celebrations. I remember our Italian grandfather sitting at the head of our long family table, pouring wine for everyone. All the women in the family were great cooks, and they each contributed their most famous dish to our feasts. And still, above all, it was the love in the family that was so nourishing.

We were not wealthy, and the clothes I wore were simple hand-medowns. And yet, we were there in Hollywood, which at that time was still very beautiful. Sunset Strip was lined with boutique shops and restaurants where famous actresses and actors sat and ate. At school, I found myself in classes with the children of movie stars, including David and Ricky Nelson

....

My education in elementary school and junior high was more about cultivating the soul than about what was in books. I don't remember much about school in the early grades, but I can vividly remember my fifth grade teacher, Mrs. Gardner. She was a gentle and sweet woman who tended children as a gardener would, bringing life to everything. In contrast, Miss Pinkerton in Grade 6 was a dried-up, unmarried matron who taught with a ruler in her hand. In her presence, I learned to see how a human being who is not fulfilled on some deep level can become bitter, almost ugly, as they get older. The ugliness begins on the inside, but it shapes the way the face looks. Miss Pinkerton's face had become the story of her bitter, unfulfilled life.

....

I loved junior high. I had good grades, achieved the honor roll and was involved in everything a young person could hope for at that time in her life. I was a pom-pom girl for the football team, and president of our graduating 9th grade class. Those years were very fulfilling for me.

Hollywood High was a different thing entirely. By the time I got to high school, I was beginning to bloom in my soul and was looking, really looking for something that confirmed an inner feeling for truth. I sought for ideals, and I was waking up to the world.

In high school, I felt like I was "doing time," as if I were in a jail with nothing more to be expected at the end than the "Good Housekeeping Stamp of Approval." What the teachers were doing and teaching had nothing to do with my own quest, or what I was doing, and wanting, and searching for. It was not working for me, and three months short of graduation, I quit. My mother was terribly disappointed when I made this decision. Five years earlier, I had done the same thing with the church. The truth is, this spirit of independence had awoken in me at the time of my father's death.

PART TWO

INDEPENDENCE AND THE YEARS IN HOLLYWOOD

The first job I had was at Grauman's Chinese Theater. I was 15 and had a false ID, pretending to be 18. Splashed across the huge cinemascope screen were images of people like Marilyn Monroe, Marlin Brando, and James Dean. I was in love with all of them, and with everything about that beautiful time. It was then that I met my future husband, Harry, a long-haired, wild and charismatic man who was trying to build a career as a singer. He epitomized all the things that were "happening" in the late 50's and the beginning of the sixties.

When I was almost 18, I moved into a small apartment in Laurel Canyon with a girlfriend. Harry and I were dating. Harry's idol, and the idol of most of the world at that time, was Frank Sinatra. He had just completed, "From Here to Eternity," a movie that revitalized his career and earned him an Oscar for Best Supporting Actor. He was married to his second wife, Ava Gardener, but during this time they were going through one of their many separations.

The Villa Capri restaurant on Yucca Street in Hollywood was owned by Frank Sinatra. I knew several of the young guys that worked there, and they told me that Sinatra occasionally came into the restaurant. "Wow," I thought, "If I could see him in person, that would be extraordinary." I was enthralled with the idea of meeting the great Frank Sinatra. One of the guys said he would call me when he knew Mr. Sinatra was going to come in. Late one afternoon I received a telephone call, telling me that he would be in that evening.

Everyone I knew had a fake I.D., and at 17 I'd already had mine for a couple of years. That evening I got really dressed up, with full make-up. I

9

looked pretty close to, if not older than 21, and mature enough to go sit at the bar at the Villa Capri. I sat there alone, ordered a drink, and positioned myself in full view of Sinatra, who was seated across the room with a group of friends. He caught my eye and we began to flirt with each other. We flirted back and forth for quite some time. After awhile, a younger man came up to me and said, "Mr. Sinatra is going to have a party at his home after he leaves the restaurant, and he would like you to come." I said, "Absolutely, but I don't have a car." My girlfriend had dropped me off and either she or one of the young guys was to drive me home. It was arranged that I would get a ride up to the house.

It was a large party, hosting probably 20 to 25 people of all ages. I especially remember one elderly couple, a very beautiful gray-haired lady with her dignified-looking husband. The party went on for several hours, and it was a lovely event, with interesting people engaged in spirited conversations. And then Frank himself came up to me and said, "Would you like to be here tonight with me?" I said, "I would love it." And so I stayed. He was not at all egotistic. He was sweet, gentle and kind, and very, very beautiful.

In the morning we woke up and had some breakfast. Then Frank said, "Do you have a car?" I told him I did not, and that I lived in Laurel Canyon. He said, "Then I'll drive you home." It was a beautiful, sunny morning. We went outside together and he showed me his car, a very fancy Karmann Ghia from Italy. He put the top down, and we drove along all the winding upper canyon roads before he took me to Laurel Canyon. At one point, he turned on the radio and his top record at that time, "Come fly with Me," started playing. There I was, seventeen years old and riding through the Hollywood Hills with Frank Sinatra in his magnificent car, with his voice blasting on the radio as he drove me home to my little house in Laurel Canyon. *I was living a dream.*

I didn't see him again after that until many, many years later, when once again I was invited to his home for a party. By that time I was involved in the film industry, and knew many other people in those circles. My dreams have obviously changed since then, but that, at that time, was very special.

When I was 19, my boyfriend Harry and I ran off to Las Vegas to secretly get married. Again: an act of independence!

Harry re-introduced me to a man named Dr. Arthur Chandler, a psychiatrist active in the very beginnings of the experimental work with LSD in the late 1950's. I had gone through three sessions with Dr. Chandler on my own several years earlier. This time, I was looking for a job and Dr. Chandler was looking for a secretary. I interviewed with him and got the job.

I worked for Dr. Chandler in Beverly Hills. He and his colleagues were all doing research work with LSD, just as Albert Hoffmann and Timothy Leary were doing on the East Coast at Harvard University. This research was conducted with the approval of the American government, and sponsored by Sandoz Pharmaceutical Company. *

People from all walks of life found their way to Dr. Chandler and his associates. Working with him, I met heroin addicts, alcoholics and movie stars. Their therapy treatments included sessions in which they were given varying dosages of LSD. These experimental sessions provided an amazing opportunity for everyone involved to explore human consciousness.

* It was whispered at that time that this experimental work with psychedelic drugs was experimented with by different people around the world. This research was given to Stanislav Grof in Czechoslovakia, Albert Hoffman and Leary at Harvard, Chandler and three others in LA. It was apparently done at the request of the US government, which was concerned that Russia had made advances in psychic research, and these were viewed as a threat to the US because of the Cold War.

People who took these doctor-administered mega-doses of drugs sometimes regressed back to the womb and beyond, into past lives. Their sessions lasted three or four hours, and one of my jobs was to sit with them afterwards while they "came down" and waited for their ride to come and pick them up. I also transcribed the reports on their sessions. This experience gave me one of the greatest insights I could ever have into human consciousness and human potential. I was 21 at the time.

With Dr. Chandler's work, I had the opportunity to realize that we have no limitations except those that have, in a certain sense, been imposed upon us through our civilization or the stages of evolution we are living in as the human race. Within every human being there lives a wonderful spark with great potential. Very few people have an opportunity to really change unless that spark at some point becomes a flame in them, a flame for truth. Yet the light is there---for everyone.

Dr. Chandler's work was a rescue mission, and under his supervision LSD helped many people in those years. I had heard about a woman named Francine. I met her and took her under my wing. She was a heroin addict with two small children. I went to her home -- it was dark, dingy, and filthy -- and I convinced her to meet Dr. Chandler, promising that he would see her at no cost. One day after a session, I walked outside with her. She looked up and said, "Oh, the sky! I have not seen the sky for such a long time!"

Francine had lived in the darkness of heroin. She was so unconscious that she could have killed herself without even knowing what she was doing. We caught her right before she could have destroyed herself, and we were able to help her and her children.

I did a lot of that kind of work at that time in my life. I was there to help wherever and however I could.

I worked as Dr. Chandler's secretary for almost one year. After I left that job, I actually went through five other LSD sessions myself. (Dr. Chandler had insisted it would have been unethical to do this while I

12

worked for him.)

I was still married to Harry at that time, but because of the work with Dr. Chandler and because of my own LSD sessions, I developed insights that allowed me to see that Harry was caught in the same destructive patterns he had been in since his teenage years. I truly loved him, but if I had stayed with him, I would have destroyed myself. I was really ready to live life in a very good way, and I simply had to move on.

It was after I separated from him that I started studying acting. The well-known actor James Coburn (The Magnificent Seven) had recommended that I study with Jeff Corey, who had starred in Orson Wells' The Third Man. I got another great apartment, started meditating, and my life changed dramatically.

. . . .

During those years I met many interesting people, including young film actors and people from the music and film world, such as Bobby "Bob" Dylan, Donovan, Peter Fonda, and Steve McQueen.

I first met Bob Dylan at Tom and John Law's Hollywood Hills home, at a grand dance party with a hundred or so upcoming stars. On this occasion, I had an opportunity to have a conversation with him. He spoke in very abstract sentences, but—in spite of the drugs he was taking---I could understand what he was saying, drawing upon what I had learned through my previous work in psychiatry, He was a true poet of the 60's, and a very talented person.

Some weeks later, we were all invited to attend a concert at the Civic Auditorium in Santa Monica. Dylan reserved the entire tenth row for the Law brothers and their friends. We arrived just before the concert was starting, and there, sitting in the middle of our reserved row, were Marlon Brando and his date. They had to be asked to move by the ushers! This was hard on his ego, and he was furious.

I also developed a social friendship with Steve McQueen. One weekend, my husband Harry and I traveled together to San Francisco with him and his first wife, Neile Adams. We played together in the city, eating, dancing, and having good conversations.

Many years passed before I had other occasions to meet Steve at Hollywood parties. One such party was at the home of Jane Fonda in Malibu, California, attended by a fantastic group of young stars, including Mia Farrow, who had just returned from India. Henry and Peter Fonda were also at the party. I found that the entire Fonda family were very gracious people, and they left a strong impression on me. They all shared a dignity that is not so often experienced amongst the Hollywood set.

PART THREE

EXPERIENCES IN THE DESERT

Out of all of my Hollywood connections, there was one person in particular who became a good friend. This was folk singer Ted Markland. He had begun his career as a stand-up satirist, managed by Lenny Bruce. Most people will remember him as the character Reno in the television western High Chaparral.

I knew Ted as a deeply spiritual man who had a profound resonance with Native American ritual and Buddhist philosophy. He would often lead friends up the desert mountains to experience consciousness-awakening, telling them, "As you're going up the mountain, you're not only going up physically, you are also going up mentally and spiritually."

Climbing with Ted was one way I was able to survive the craziness of Hollywood. Sometimes just the two of us went there together. He would go off on one hill and I would stay on another, and we would watch the stars all night long. When morning came, I loved to look out over the desert. I consciously exercised my ability to perceive as much as possible, looking as far into the distance as I could. Then I would close my eyes and do the same thing with my hearing. I felt as though my whole body became a listening ear, and I could hear for miles and miles in the desert stillness. These experiences helped me begin to unlock what I believe is a potential for every human being, namely, the ability to penetrate with our organs of perception into dimensions of reality that we don't even stop to consider in our everyday life. We need to learn to develop this ability through mind-exercise, because it does not develop without practice.

The Deserts: they are sacred for me. They have been my biographical thread from that first moment in the Painted Desert when I awoke alone in my parents' car as a small child. The deserts of New Mexico and

Arizona, the high deserts of Southern California, the deserts of Egypt--they have all given me profound experiences and spiritual portals.

Through our desert experiences, Ted Markland became my spiritual brother, my sensitive guide. He influenced how I walked and moved my body in peace in the desert, even with rattlesnakes. Ted taught me how, when our feet touch the earth, our energy penetrates through it in all directions. That energy radiates directly from what lives in our hearts and our minds into the Earth and into the world. If there is a rattlesnake close by, it feels that energy and whether it is in harmony or is negative or aggressive. The war with the snake is declared long before you come into physical contact with it.

Once, coming down the mountain, Ted met a family of rattlesnakes. They were right on his path. He took out his flute and played music to them, and they allowed him to pass. What the Native Americans tell us is this: *"Everything is Spirit. If you are truly one in spirit with something, even something you would ordinarily consider dangerous, the dualistic Separation has been bridged, and there is, therefore, no danger."*

. . . .

In the late summer of 1966, Ted invited me to join him and an upcoming film star, John Law (known from the movie "The Russians are Coming! The Russians are Coming!") to spend time with the Navajo and Hopi Indians on their reservations. We drove into the deserts and visited the Navajos first. There we were invited to stay in the home of Robert, the medicine man of the tribe. The United States border between Arizona and New Mexico ran right through the middle of his house. In the Navajo nation, of course, the distinctions drawn according to White Man's geography had no significance.

Robert lived in a hogan, together with his wife and children. We stayed several nights with them, sleeping in a circle with all the beds pointing towards the wall--children, young braves, Ted, John, and me. During the days, I played with the children, went out with the sheep and did many things that allowed me to touch something primal and non-dualistic in

16

my soul. Something in me was awakened through this experience, something that remembered I had lived there before.

We journeyed to the Navajos because we had been invited to join them in their peyote church. In Los Angeles, I had known several people who had gone to peyote meetings, including a friend who had been very ill. The people of the tribe placed him in the center of the teepee and devoted a whole meeting to him and his healing. They directed their spirit energy toward him, and they healed him. When so many people pour their loving devotion toward one person, it can have a profound effect.

Peyote is one of the most difficult things a person could ever ingest. Because it contains four known poisons, including cyanide at a very minute level, peyote actually purges the body and the soul. A person can initially get very sick to the stomach.

In the morning of the peyote church meeting, we took some peyote in a powder form to prepare ourselves for the ceremonies that would begin that evening. I was told to hold it in my mouth and to pray with it for at least one hour. I rolled it around in my mouth and made a ball of saliva around it. The saliva helped to digest the powder, so it was important to enfold it as much as possible. This preparatory stage was meant to cleanse away all impurities, all the things that stood in the way, and to overcome the terrible bitter taste.

That afternoon, we climbed up into the hills and rocks around the reservation. I went to one place where I sat completely alone, choosing a place in the sun that was warm, wonderful, and divine. I had gone to the reservation with a deep question about my destiny path, and as I sat there alone, the answer began to take form. I had come to the Navajo because I wanted to have the experience of the Native American and how they lived in relationship with Spirit. I was drawn to this path because I felt totally at home in it. I knew it in my bones. When I walked in the desert, my feet could hear the rhythms and songs of the people. The Earth would sing the songs of the past and I could sing and hum along with them. But I had also learned of the works of Austrian

17

philosopher Rudolf Steiner. Even though the ideas, intellectual spirituality and academic demands of his Anthroposophy were absolutely foreign to me, I felt drawn to them as well, and knew that this would be a next step in my destiny!

That sunny afternoon, sitting alone on a rock above the Navajo reservation, the answer to my question flooded my soul and I understood something. The Native American path was already within me. I had lived it somewhere in a past incarnation and the vivid images of that past were always with me. The works of Steiner were not a part of that spiritually remembered path, but they were what I needed for the future. I knew that if I chose to study his teachings, it would mean adventuring into the unknown, maybe even moving to Europe and giving up the Hollywood life I had worked for--including an imminent film career. But on that afternoon, I knew that this was something I had to look at on a much deeper level.

That evening, we all went to the church of the Navajo. Everyone walked in quietly and took their places in the large teepee. Sitting across from me were women who were over one hundred years old. Their eyes were steady and bright, and their faces shone with ancient beauty. They wore round turquoise, coral, and silver discs around their necks--huge, magnificent mandalas. There were many young braves there, as well as children. We all sat cross-legged on the floor for twelve hours.

The Navajo have distrust for the White race, justifiably so. But they trusted Ted, calling him Brother and inviting him to sing and play flute during their ceremonies. They saw Ted with no barrier or limitation of race. They were color-blind to him; they saw only his spirit. I was the third white woman to be allowed to participate in one of their ceremonies, because he brought me there and had a strong friendship with Robert, the medicine man.

During that six hour period, from early evening to midnight, tribal members passed around three forms of peyote: a brewed tea, a powder which is dried peyote ground very fine, and the raw buttons, which are almost like artichoke hearts, but with a very bitter taste. Singing and drumming filled the air. As the evening approached midnight, I experienced people singing, joining their voices in sublime song. The voices sounded as though they were coming from the heavens above, pouring down into the singers.

At midnight we took a break. Someone suggested that we go out in twos because the desert was very black. I suddenly realized that I was the only one left sitting there. There was no one to accompany me into that dark night. Actually, I wasn't sure if I could stand up. I had been sitting for six hours and I had taken a lot of peyote. But when I did stand up, I felt myself totally in my body, and absolutely certain about the way I took every step. When I got to the opening of the teepee, two old, native women standing just outside asked me, "Will you be okay going out there all alone?" I said, "Yes."

I stepped away from the teepee and was immediately engulfed in the desert midnight. I could not see my hand in front of my face. As I walked out into the blackness and looked up to the brilliance of the heavens and the light that filled the sky, I became aware of the great light energy of the cosmos. Knowing my spirit as part of that energy field opened my human instrument. The light energy poured itself through my being, just as the music had poured itself through those who were singing in the circle of the peyote meeting. My eyes then became the instrument that projected light onto the desert floor, lighting my path. I could see everywhere I went. It was as though I had a flashlight. When I walked back to the teepee, the two old women were waiting to embrace me and to accept me into the tribe.

Just before dawn, we all got up to receive the sunrise. The fire was out. The chimney had been removed and the beginnings of the dawn glowed through the opening. Where the fire had been, a dove of peace now stood, created from out of the night's ashes by members of the tribe.

We all went outside and, climbing in different directions, reached the surrounding peaks and greeted the sunrise. When we returned, we found that the women had prepared a feast. We all ate together, and spent the rest of the day at the hogan.

We left the next day. As we drove away I reflected on my experiences and one especially was very funny. They had a row of outhouses and none had doors. I remember how I sat in one of the houses, and someone walked by and simply greeted me as though I was waiting for a bus! I also realized that during the entire week I had never seen a mirror, and that I had not needed one. Living in that state gave a great sense of freedom from vanity and ego. Everything was just what it was; there was no vanity.

Through these "mind altering" experiences, I learned to touch greater dimensions of consciousness. All of these experiences could not have been revealed if those levels were not inherently within the human consciousness. These substances alter the mind so that spirit can be experienced, freeing the mind from brain-bound constraints. These experiences led me now to seek a path where I could develop this same *seeing*, without the use of psychedelics.

. . . .

From the Navajo reservation, Ted, John and I drove to Hopi Land. Ted knew the head medicine man from the second mesa in that Nation, David Monongye, known to his people as "Grandfather David." He invited us into his home, and his wife prepared us a fine meal that we all enjoyed together.

Grandfather David told us about a healing ceremony he had done the night before. As he spoke, he told us how his people had ascended out of the Grand Canyon floor from Atlantis. This was the first time I had heard the word "Atlantis." The power of that word struck my backbone; it was something I *knew*. Words matter. They are registered in our DNA.

David Monongye was a very tall man. Archetypally Native American, he had high cheekbones and a magnificent radiance. Years later I heard that he had been invited to speak at the United Nations as the representative of all the tribes in the United States.

Kivas, which are round mud huts looking a little bit like beehives, represent different aspects of Hopi religion. Each kiva represents a certain spirit-being. Grandfather David was in charge of the Rattlesnake Kiva, which stood along with other kivas on the second mesa. He and young braves collected rattlesnakes in the desert with their bare hands and brought them to the Rattlesnake Kiva, where they performed ceremonial dances with them. They knew no fear, no dualism; they experienced pure spirit existing between themselves and the snake. These native people had absolutely nothing, not even a veil, between their spirit and the spirit of any other thing. They were one with all sentient beings, with no separation.

The White Man lost the privilege of attending these ceremonies, because they insisted on taking flash photographs or engaging in other misbehaviors which startled the snakes who would then strike. Soon, the White Man was not allowed to attend any ceremony. They simply could not align themselves energetically to be in tune with what the Native Americans were doing ceremonially.

For many years afterwards, Grandfather David came to me in my meditations. Whenever I needed guidance, there was always a greater being who appeared in my mind's eye, giving me wisdom and advice. To have such a knowing in the core of what you believe, to know the connection that exists between all Spirit with no doubt and no compromise; this is to achieve freedom from dualistic thinking. This achievement must be won over and over again.

PART FOUR

MY MEETING WITH ANTHROPOSOPHY

In 1966 and 1967, four significant people appeared in my life: Douglas Gunkel, Edith Gutterson, Dr. Siegfried Knauer, and Willi Sucher. Each of them introduced me to a facet of the work of Rudolf Steiner, and the thoughts of Anthroposophy.

My friend Douglas Gunkel was an artist who lived in Joshua Tree. He was invited to have an exhibition of his works in Burbank, California by Edith Gutterson, a woman who had previously been an art critic at the Modern Museum of Art in New York.

When I met Edith at the exhibition, I learned that she was studying Anthroposophy, the life work of Rudolf Steiner. I discovered that there were quite a few other people present who were also studying Anthroposophy, and many of them were involved in the arts. One of them in particular was a producer and director of plays, and because of my own studies in theater arts, he invited me to audition for the lead role in "The Lady is not for Burning" by Christopher Frye. I auditioned and got the lead role. It was this that opened the door to the next chapter of my life.

Some of the other actors in the production were also involved in Anthroposophy. One day, one of them, a young woman named Linda Killian, invited me to join her in a class of something called "Eurythmy," which she told me was a form of classical movement inspired by Rudolf Steiner. This was my introduction to what would become my future profession.

Edith was already quite old when I first met her. Through my encounters with her, I experienced an important change in the way I saw older people. Her insights and words had such a profound effect on me that I wanted to know *what* she knew. I spent time with her, preparing meals, accompanying her to appointments, and learning simply from her wise presence. She also helped me see my ability to heal with my hands, something I had never realized before.

When I asked Edith how I could learn more about Anthroposophy, she told me that I should seek out a man named Willi Sucher, who had known Rudolf Steiner personally. She told me much about him, but it wasn't until her death in 1967 that I was able to meet him personally.

....

Edith had suffered from cancer earlier in her life. The doctors who worked with standard medicine told her that the cancer was too advanced for her to have an operation. Edith was unwilling to accept this verdict without question, and so she turned to her personal physician, Dr. Siegfried Knauer, who worked with anthroposophical medicine. Even though he was not a surgeon, she had full confidence in him, and asked him to perform the surgery needed to remove the tumor. He did so successfully, and she lived another twenty years,

Not long after I met Edith, she had an opportunity to introduce me to Dr. Knauer. LA was rolling in its smog bath in the 60's, and one season I developed such a miserable sinus infection that I couldn't breathe at all. Edith introduced me to Dr. Knauer, and, although he was not taking new patients, he agreed to see me the next morning before regular office hours. I lay on the examination table in his office, and he examined me by moving his hands six or seven inches above my body. At one point, I opened my eyes and saw him working with a pendulum. He identified the source of my problem and then selected a few possible remedies from among hundreds of little bottles on the shelves. He tested them by placing each one directly on the ill area of my body. Working like an alchemist, he then identified the appropriate medicines and mixed them right in front of me.

I had expected that he would treat my sinuses directly because they were so congested, but in fact the remedy he gave me was for my blocked kidneys. He explained that they needed help because they were not able to filter fluids out of my body. Some days later, my sinuses were clear and I was breathing freely.

After Dr. Knauer gave me these medicines, I asked him if there were not also another way to work on my healing from the consciousness plane. He then gave me meditations to work with, explaining that for true healing to occur, illnesses must be worked on from two directions. Things that are manifest on the physical plane must be worked on not only from the physical plane, but also from the spiritual plane; that is to say, one must address not only the cause, but also the effect.

Siegfried Knauer was more than a mere physician; he was a true healer. Born in Kiev, Russia, to German diplomatic parents, he was educated in Germany and spoke many languages. He was an extraordinarily advanced physician, and even his European peers considered him a genius, for he perceived illnesses and healing from their origins. As I came to know him over the course of many years, he led me to the understanding that true medicine, true healing, was hardly being practiced in the world today, and certainly not in America or Europe. He helped me to realize that a doctor's primary tool is his own consciousness, and that he can only heal as fully as his own conscious awareness has been developed.

We don't have many, if any, true healers in the medical professions in this country. Typically, doctors in the US rely on diagnostic information obtained from machines. There are carefully trained and often highly sensitive diagnosticians in the West, but even those who diagnose correctly often don't know how to heal holistically. Even when they prescribe medicines, the negative side effects can easily undo their benefits. To put it very simply: very few practitioners of conventional (allopathic) medicine understand healing.

. . . .

After my encounter with Anthroposophy and these truly inspiring people, I began to question the whole premise of having a film career. I had little, if any, illusion about the film industry. As I watched different friends, including James Coburn, Steve McQueen, Ted Markland and others become big stars, I saw how they changed, and began to identify with their personalities. I could experience that the image they played on the screen became their reality, and that they were lost without all the personality props. I attended parties, including one at Richard Burton and Elizabeth Taylor's home following "Who's Afraid of Virginia Woolf?" and saw even beautiful Taylor with a strange emptiness in her eyes.

All this was discouraging for me, and in fact helped me to make the decision not to make this my profession, even though I loved acting, especially on the stage.

My last film interview in Hollywood was an audition with the man who was then president of Warner Brothers. I prepared the last scene from Joan of Arc by George Bernard Shaw. I loved Joan and put my whole being into this scene. The president was so impressed with my performance that he got another person to come in and witness my presentation, and then told me that he wanted to find a film that could allow me to be "introduced" to the public. With this imminent career before me I began to really ask myself, "Is this what I really want???" And the resounding answer was "NO!"

And so it was that I decided instead to move to Europe to begin a brand new artistic training, either in painting or in eurythmy. I began selling everything I owned, including things I had made and artwork I had bought.

One weekend I planned a garage sale. My whole apartment was in disarray because people had been in and out all day; some things were moved around and other things had been sold. I was preparing to leave within a couple of weeks.

That evening some friends called and invited me to go out to dinner with them. I readily agreed, and hurried out of the house to meet them. It was midnight by the time they dropped me off back at my apartment.

As they drove off, I realized I had left home without my handbag. I had no keys! And I had just that day sold the statue that hid my stash key on the front porch.

The only way that I could get in to this apartment was through a skylight on the roof. I climbed the fence, managed to get up onto the roof, pried open the skylight, and jumped down into my room. Having had a lot of movement and gymnastic practice my entire life, I did not even question that I might get hurt. That is the way of the youthful mind.

The pain I felt when I landed was excruciating. My ankles immediately swelled up so much that I had to struggle to pull my boots off. There was no one I could call at that hour, so I lay awake in bed all night, with one ankle fractured and the other one ripped apart. I didn't know what to do. Then I thought about young boys in Vietnam on the front lines, lying on the ground with their legs or their arms blown off. I found I was able to direct my field of awareness towards them, towards others who were suffering far more than I was. I had so much compassion for them that I managed to make it through that night and bear it. I was 28 years old.

I managed to get to the doctor the next day. My ankles were so swollen that he couldn't tell me if anything was broken or not. Nonetheless, I told him, "It doesn't matter what it is, I am leaving for Europe."

I bandaged my ankles and my feet and had little leather sandals made that I could wear with the bandages. I was on crutches for a while. By my departure date, I was able to hobble onto the plane.

I had meditated deeply about my decision to leave LA and move to Europe. The truth of my next step was apparent to me on a deep, deep level of my soul. It was a spiritual awakening so strong that I was able to leave behind my family, friends, lover, home, and budding career. To this day I can vividly remember my promise to myself as that plane flew over Los Angeles: "I will never come back here unless God himself wills it."

I arrived in Germany in the summer of 1968. I had paid off all my debts, and everything I owned was in a trunk that I had shipped. It was a new canvas.

I began by traveling through Europe, visiting several schools to find a place where I could study. One of the important centers of learning was in Dornach, Switzerland, near Basel, where Rudolf Steiner had created a center for the Anthroposophical work. After spending one week there, I realized that this was the place I could meet my next step in destiny. I chose one of the Eurythmy schools there, and enrolled.

I had to wait for several months before the new school year would begin, so I first took a job at the Ita Wegman Clinic, an anthroposophical/ homeopathic clinic (we would call it a hospital in this country) near Dornach. There I trained as a nurse's aide in a cancer ward. I could immediately see how different this clinic was from those in the United States, and how differently the patients were treated. For instance, doctors prescribed different arts for the patients in pre- and post-operative stages of illnesses. Some patients' were prescribed musical therapy, while others needed painting, and still others sculpture. All the patients were prescribed eurythmy therapy. It was a great experience for me to be able to enter this absolutely wonderful world of medicine.

As we moved through autumn and into winter, the weather got cold. California girl that I was, I didn't know how to dress for cold weather and I quickly caught a potent flu. My fever spiked so high I started hallucinating. I soon found myself in ancient Egypt, both with my eyes open and with my eyes closed, I was enveloped in ancient Egypt. My fever was so high that I was admitted to the clinic where the staff worked to bring it down. But because of that illness, I decided that I had to go to Egypt.

....

When I had been living in LA. I had had a period of about six months during which I dreamed about Egypt all the time. I had worked on a large 3' by 5' collage, focusing on the theme of Egypt. When I completed and sold the piece, the dreams stopped. Now, however, I knew the time had come for me to go there. I called my family to tell them, and my older sister said she would go with me. That winter, during Christmas break, my sister, my friend Karen and I left for this great ancient land.

In the Middle East, planes often arrive in the middle of the night when runways are cool. We didn't really see anything of the sights of Egypt until the next day, when we flew to Aswan. In the morning, I walked across the room where we were staying, and opened the shutters wide. We could see the Nile! And in that moment I felt in the core of my being that I was *home*.

We travelled north to Luxor, to visit the Valley of the Kings. There the pharaohs of old were buried in magnificent underground tombs. The dry air of the desert has preserved the vibrant colors of the murals in the ancient tombs, and one could still read the hieroglyphs that had been painted there long ago.

Death, as we know it, did not exist for the ancient Egyptians, for what we call death was simply a passage for them. All of the hieroglyphs in all of the tunnels were descriptions of the rituals surrounding that passage. The dead one was showered with gifts and food to accompany him or her on their journey to the Afterlife.

The most impressive tomb was that of Tutankhamen. We entered his tomb and walked down the long passageway, covered with murals. There, I sat by his sarcophagus and thought, "They can just close up the tomb and leave me here." I felt a deep connection to Tutankhamen and began reading about him. The deep remembering in the unfolding of that present moment took me far back into ancient times. My cells *remembered*. There was no question in my mind about reincarnation, or that I had been a part of that Egyptian culture, many times. It was all familiar to me.

. . . .

After this wonderful trip, we journeyed back to Switzerland and my sister returned to Palm Springs, CA. I continued studying eurythmy but I felt so unhappy and frustrated with my training and the way that I was being taught that I truly questioned what my next step should be. I considered looking for a different school, or even beginning a different study. I had left the United States when I was 28, at the threshold of a budding film character. I had experienced the ways and wisdom of the Navajo and Hopi Native Americans, and I had worked with Dr. Chandler on the LSD research project. Now I was studying Eurythmy, because I recognized so clearly that it is a path of initiation. It was hard for me to bear the fact that some of the other students were not taking this study to the depths that were intended, and the work we did in the classes was not satisfying.

I remained at this school for two years, but my questions remained. Had I misunderstood the potential of this training? Perhaps I was mistaken: maybe what I was learning was all there was to learn. But something in me knew there was something more, something other than what I was being taught, something much more profound. I knew this with deep certainty, even though this was not what was being taught in this school.

Upon the advice of a friend, I decided to go and talk to Ilona Schubert, an elderly eurythmist who had been trained by Rudolf Steiner himself. I hoped she could offer me the advice I needed. I knocked on her door, and when it opened I was met by a tiny, angelic-looking woman in her 70's. In my hand I carried a bouquet of sunflowers to give to her because I had heard that her husband had only very recently died. She was holding a three-day vigil for him in her home, and invited me to go with her into the room where his coffin stood. We stood there together, looking at him quietly.

Then she spoke. "A most unusual thing happened just five days before Gunter died. Suddenly, he started speaking to me in English. He had never spoken to me in English before, although he was a linguist and spoke many languages. I asked him, 'Why do you speak to me in English, Gunter?' He said, "You are going to need it soon, my dear.'"

Ilona and I made a very strong connection, and I began studying eurythmy with her shortly thereafter. From my very first lesson with her,

I knew that she was teaching me what I was looking for, which was not what I was getting at the school. And that really gave me something to think about: "What is it in us that truly *knows*, in a primal way? That *knows*, even if we have not had any exposure in our daily lives to anything with which we could compare, where we could even see a difference, where there is not even a possibility for comparison?" I realized: that part of us that can *intuit* always knows truth.

I decided I would finish the term at school and study with her on the side. At the end of that semester, I made a clear decision to dedicate myself to studying with her as my teacher, and withdrew from the school. I worked with her and another colleague of hers who had also been trained by Steiner. They did not teach me through mere imitation, as I had been taught in the school; they gave me tools through a cognitive process, showing me how to realize something at a high level and then translate it into the body. This kind of teaching enables the student to arrive at the source of learning, and become a teacher for one's own self.

I studied in Switzerland for six years. After four years of artistic training, I organized a performing tour for the western US. Then I returned to Switzerland for two further years of training in therapeutic eurythmy.

. . . .

During this time, my Norwegian boyfriend, who was studying speech in Dornach, became ill and unable to use his legs as a result of a live polio vaccine he had been given as a child. I became his caregiver, and worked intensively with him. Together, we went to visit Frau DeJagger, the first Therapeutic Eurythmist who had been trained personally by Dr. Rudolf Steiner, Dr. Ita Wegman, and Marie Steiner. I observed how she worked with him, doing eurythmy directly on his heart, and I practiced with her so that I could continue with him alone at home.

Though this woman was old and blind, she continued to teach, and many students went to her curative eurythmy courses. I attended one workshop that was so full we had to stand in three circles around her.

31

One day, as she was reciting the first lines of the Gospel of St. John which was her personal meditation, she walked slowly around the students. As she got closer to me, I made a great effort to expand myself with energy, even though I knew she was blind and couldn't see me. But as she came near to me, she exclaimed, "No, no, no! You just had it, and you just lost it! What did you do?"

Eurythmy is a spiritual art of movement. It works with the laws of invisible etheric life forces, the energetic forces closest to the physical body. That moment with Frau DeJagger became one of the most important lessons in Eurythmy I have ever had; indeed, one of the most important lessons in my life. She was totally blind physically, yet she saw my etheric life forces spiritually. She saw me move from purely *being* the eurythmy sound to *exerting* personal effort to try to make it happen. She perceived me moving from the selfless pure state into the ego state.

. . . .

My six years' study in Switzerland, which gave me fantastic opportunities to perform and teach around the world, was the equivalent of a masters' degree in fine arts. It was a deep and thorough study of movement, language arts, and music. Much later, I realized in retrospect that when I carefully chose this path of study in the late 60's, I did so because it allowed me to unite my own inner language with an objective terminology of spiritual truths. These "language skills" tools gave me the ability to articulate in words the things I had been perceiving since I was very young. All the rich experiences in my life now had a true language, a voice. This could unfold through the study of Anthroposophy, the work of Steiner, which gives western civilization a language to describe cognitive ideas. It gives feet and legs to ideas, and creates the possibility of transformation in the arts, medicine, horticulture, sciences, and education, to name just a few of the many fields of anthroposophically-inspired work.

At the end of my studies, I had the opportunity to go to Greece with two of my girlfriends who had also just graduated. We were there less than a week when war broke out with Turkey and we were asked to leave the country. I absolutely refused. I had waited a long time to travel to Greece and no one was going to force me to leave. We stayed in a hotel by the airport and waited while the battles continued. This was, fortunately, a small war sparked by a land dispute, and it quickly resolved. When the conflict was resolved a week later, we were practically the only tourists left.

We drove all over the islands. We drove through villages where the women had sat on their porches dressed all in black at the outbreak of war, all of them weeping. They resembled the archetypal Trojan women weeping the grief of war, the suffering of watching their loved ones leave and go into danger, possibly never to return. It is always the women and the children who are left to suffer alone. This is the futility of war, continuing down through antiquity to the present moment.

We drove through this present moment antiquity--Athens, Delphi, Sparta, Epidaurus--and when we returned to Switzerland, it was time to return to California and start the next chapter of my life.

PART FIVE

A NEW LIFE IN CALIFORNIA

When I was living in Los Angeles, my friend Edith Gutterson told me that if I was interested in learning more about the studies she was interested in, I should seek out her friend Willi Sucher. As it turned out, it was only at Edith's funeral in 1967 that I was able to meet him. Over the course of the next decades, he became a very important person in my life.

Willi had been a banker in Stuttgart, Germany when Rudolf Steiner was alive, and as a young man worked as a teller in the bank which Steiner frequented. He had intuited the dangers in Hitler's rise to power in the 1930's and emigrated to England when the threat of war was imminent. During the war he was interred in a German nationals' encampment on the Isle of Man. There he met Dr. Karl König, the founder of the Camp Hill movement for handicapped individuals, as well as several other students of Anthroposophy.

Willi's spiritual interests led him, with his vast skills as a mathematician, to begin studying the mathematical relationship-patterns in the movements of the planets. He worked closely together with Dr. Elizabeth Vreede, a close student of Steiner, and together they developed "Astrosophy," a spiritual astrology grounded in these astronomical planetary patterns. This became Willi's life work.

When I was planning my return to the States, I knew I wanted to live in a community context with someone whose life work had led to the growth of wisdom within them. I learned that Willi and his wife Helen had moved to the Sierra Foothills in Northern California, and, since Willi was the wisest person I knew in my life then, I prepared to find a home near him, in Meadow Vista, California.

I stayed in Willi and Helen's guest room until I found the perfect rental -- a four- bedroom house with a living room large enough to hold eurythmy classes. Then, together with two colleagues, I started preparing to open a school of eurythmy. In no time at all, we had six students enrolled in a four-year program.

. . . .

The next four years were a whirlwind of activity. Not only were we involved in teaching our students, but we also frequently traveled around California to give workshops and performances. Many interesting people came into my life during those years.

On one of these weekend performance/teaching trips, I missed my flight out of LA International because of beach traffic. Six hours later, I was on the midnight flight north to Sacramento. The plane's engines were still running when we boarded. I entered at the front of the plane to stay as far away from the smoking section as I could, and noticed a man who had papers spread out on two seats. His back was to me. I called to him but he couldn't hear me over the engine noise, so I tapped him on the back. He turned around, clasped my hand, and said, "Can I help you?" I asked if the seat was free and he pointed to two, saying, "Both of these are free." Just then another passenger walked by and said, "Hello, Governor Brown."

I looked straight at him and said, "That's who you are! I always knew I was going to meet you."

Returning my gaze, he replied, "You did, did you? Well. What do you do?"

I answered, "I do something called eurythmy."

"That's connected to the Waldorf Schools, isn't it? and to Steiner's work?" he said.

I was very impressed that the governor of California was so well-informed about Waldorf Schools, and so when he insisted that I sit next

36

to him, I took a seat. We talked for the entire flight. A real friendship grew out of that, and after Friedemann and I were married some years later, the two of them became friends as well. We continued to meet at social events after that, and sometimes even ran into one another at out-of-the-way places, seemingly by accident.

In Jerry Brown, I met a man who was more than a politician: he was a truly upright human being. For instance, in 1980, during his term of office as governor, California was inundated by the Mediterranean fruit fly. This happened at the end of his eight-year term as governor and just before he was going to run for the US Senate. Jerry wanted to eradicate the medflies without spraying the state with toxic chemicals, and asked the federal government to send sterile medflies. Sterile medflies would breed and wipe out the population in one or two generations, which, in the case of the medfly, would be accomplished in as few as ten days. This was a bold and noble decision. However, it appeared that fertile medflies were shipped instead, because the population tripled in a very short time, which made the epidemic much worse than it had originally been. As a result, the state was then heavily sprayed, and Jerry Brown lost his senate bid, and his political career suffered for a number of years.

When Jerry Brown retreated from public office, he purchased an old, abandoned warehouse in Oakland, close to the Bay. He lived in one section of it and used the rest as a workspace. Once a week he opened his doors, loaded tables with food and fed the homeless and others who needed food. He also hosted a radio program in Oakland, interviewing well-known thinkers such as Noam Chomsky. He was simply an exceptional, generous man, and one of the few politicians whose humanness was more important than his career.

. . . .

Our small eurythmy school continued to grow, and after eighteen months we added a second course. One year later we prepared to open a third course, and began to receive many inquiries. It was in that season that I first met my future husband, Friedemann Schwarzkopf, who came to our home in 1977 to visit the school and see about being a student.

Friedemann was a German scholar and philosopher. He had been studying at Emerson College in England, and that winter he traveled to the United States on a speaking tour with Francis Edmunds, a teacher and lecturer from that school. They toured the East Coast and Canada, and then came to Sacramento. Friedemann had heard people say that what we were doing in my school was different from most eurythmy schools. He called and scheduled an interview with me. I remember thinking when I met him, "He's so *German*, so formal and aristocratic. I cannot imagine him being in California."

However, there was still space for one more student in the upcoming class and Friedemann was interested in joining us. First, however, he had to accompany Mr. Edmunds back to England. I received a call from him the next day from London, and he told me his intention and asked if he could join the class in April--two months later--to give himself time to settle his affairs in England. I was very principled about everything I did and I said, "No. If you want to be in the course, you have to start with us on Monday." He joined us on Tuesday. He missed the first day, but he came.

The school was in session from February to June, and then had a summer holiday. Friedemann went to Europe for the summer and when he returned to California in September, he came back with a ring. I accepted his proposal and we were married on December 17, 1978.

We honeymooned over Christmas in a beautiful little village in southern France where he owned a small house. Through our courtship and marriage, I felt a bit as if he were a prince who had come and carried me off on a white horse. That's what life felt like with him.

Friedemann did everything with honor and respect, with great care and intelligence. In this, he was a very different kind of human being from others I had known. He was very formal, and a true scholar. The conversations we could have together reached depths I had not experienced with anyone before.

. . . .

38

1978 brought other changes with it as well, and we found it was time to close the eurythmy training as it had been so far. In February of 1979 a group of students graduated, and the rest of them went on to join other trainings in Europe. A few months later, Friedemann and I moved into our new home, a few miles further up the mountain than my previous place. The new piece of land was large enough that it would be possible to build a eurythmy studio there in the future. Friedemann believed in the work deeply, and was committed to supporting it. Then, in early spring we left California, to take whatever time we needed to make a long, slow trip around the world.

My maternal grandparents, Josef and Angelina Mosca, 1928, in New York.

My father, Norman Moore, 1946

My mother, Mary Mosca Moore, 1931

My early years

Christmas in California with my mother and two sisters

My sisters Barbara Teresa, Geraldine Marie and me

45

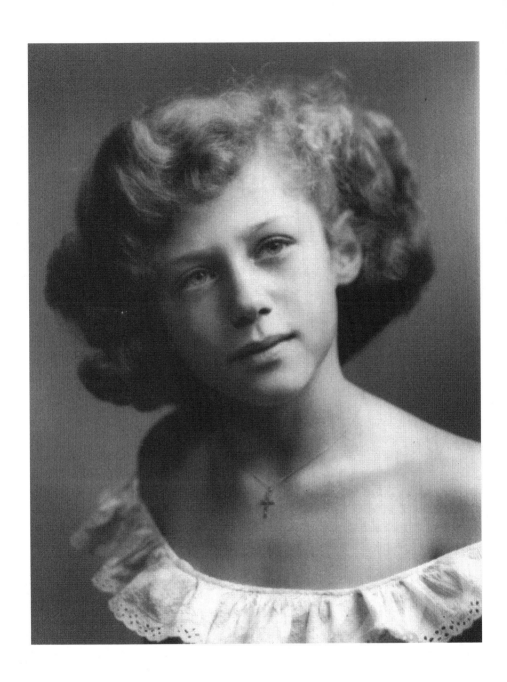

Studio photo, age 9

46

From my portfolio, age 16

Portraits from my acting portfolio (1)

Portraits from my acting portfolio (2)

Friedemann Schwarzkopf, 1947-2003

A festival during the years of the Eurythmy
training in California, spring 1978

Two bodies, one soul

PART SIX

SEEING THE WORLD

ISRAEL

Our honeymoon trip began with a trip to middle Europe. We then traveled on to the Middle East to visit the holy sites in Israel. As I approached the altar of the Greek Orthodox Chapel in Jerusalem, contained within the great Church of the Holy Sepulcher, I prepared myself to reach down through an opening in the floor to touch the rock where Jesus's body had been laid after his crucifixion. As I reached down, there was a feeling that rushed all the way through my body and struck my spine like a lightning bolt strikes a tree. This feeling was so powerful that it led me to tears, and I cried for many hours.

The effects of the event still permeated this rock. Perhaps what I was experiencing was also the energy that imbues the rock as a result of the energy and thought-forms of the tens of thousands of people who make a pilgrimage to visit it each month. In either case, the experience was powerful, and I actually believe the first scenario to be the truth. Rocks are the oldest beings on our planet, and hold deep memories.

THE FAR EAST

Friedemann and I both knew from the beginning of our personal relationship that a girl child wanted to come to us, and so we agreed that on this trip we would not travel to any lands that required me to have inoculations. This included many places in southeast Asia, which would otherwise have interested us. Friedemann had hoped to go next to India, but I had never had a real wish to go there. We were, however, both interested in meeting the Tibetan people, so we decided to go to Nepal, which would give us an opportunity to visit the Tibetan community in exile.

I had felt a deep connection to the Tibetan people ever since 1959, when I had read about the Chinese invasion of Tibet. I remember sitting alone at the table in my mother's kitchen, reading Life magazine. My mother and sister had gone to bed, and I sat there alone and wept. This was the first time in my life that I had been made aware of such cruelty. It was beyond my capability at that age to hold those things in my heart; I wept to the depth of my soul. It was very hard for me to know that human beings could be that cruel to other human beings. I remember that night to this very day: my tears, the kitchen, the table where I sat.

Friedemann was my own personal tour guide to Nepal. He had studied Eastern religions and was able to explain every single statue, every mudra, every temple. As we travelled together, I was continually astounded by his brilliant mind.

After Nepal, we continued our journey eastward, and went to Japan. There we traveled to Tokyo, Kyoto, and Nara, Japan's capital in the 6th century. In some places, we stayed in the traditional Japanese inns known as *ryokans*, furnished with tatami mats, futons, and hot tubs. During the days we visited Japan's profoundly beautiful temples.

One of the wonderful experiences of that trip was seeing how unexpected and inexplicable meetings often occurred with certain people. As we traveled through Japan's cities we kept encountering a lovely young American woman, often at temples we were visiting. And in Kamakura, where our friend Professor Takahashi had organized a eurythmy workshop for me, she appeared as a student in the class! What is the probability of encountering the same person in three different cities within a few short weeks? Some people would call this a connection of destiny or karma.

Through teaching Eurythmy in Japan, I had profound experiences of how Eurythmy can make visible the different kinds of consciousness that people in the world experience, as it is expressed through their language. Eurythmy is a kind of miracle when it is rightly understood. It is a glorious study; not just a study of movement, but a study of consciousness through movement. Language--how it is formed, how the words are spoken--forms the human being at a very early age.

As I taught the Japanese students how to create the body movements for the sounds of the vowels in Eurythmy, I experienced that the women could not participate freely. They did not have the ability to open their arms in "AH"...in AWE. They held their upper arms as if glued to their sides, and were only able to open their forearms.

I worked intensely with them to try to find a neutral, or "free" point that they could access in their souls, where they would not be paralyzed by the male/female duality that had been bred into them since birth. I had the impression that what was holding them so tightly was in their DNA, in the cells of their bodies; it was as if they not only had no freedom but also no idea that they had no freedom.

I worked intensely in the early morning session to bring them to a level of awareness that would enable them to open their arms wide and fully, from their hearts. I allowed them to work from the inside out.

We began by making small "ah's," learning to feel the gesture of opening the arms almost as if they were as fine as the petals of a rose, and then closing them again. With courage, they began opening a little bit more each time, opening and closing--contracting back into themselves and then expanding out into the world until their arms were completely freed.

Through this, I was able to witness that no matter what a person's orientation is, no matter what his or her deepest beliefs are, something primal and true lives at the core of every single person. These sounds-- and "AH" is a primal sound--are something we have had since the moment of beginning. These first sounds are an integral part of the human being.

This is the language of Eurythmy. And the speaking of language in Eurythmy is so beautiful because every single movement is a conscious movement incorporating the entire cosmic world.

Following our trip to Japan, I told Friedemann, "I can't travel anymore. I can't sleep in any more hotels, I can't eat any more restaurant food." So from Japan we returned to California and our home in Peaceful Valley.

. . . .

During our travels through the Far East, Friedemann and I experienced many wonderful cultures. Yet gradually, the impulse to build a new center for Eurythmy in California began to take root. But what should it look like?

The inspiration for the building had come during our visit to Nepal. One of the hotels we stayed in there had once been a palace. It was very beautiful, with elegant architectural lines. One day Friedemann and I were lying in the room talking when Friedemann suddenly jumped up off the bed, got down on the floor with paper and pen, and started drawing something.

And then he showed me what he had drawn and said, "This is going to be your next Eurythmy building."

Once we returned to our home in California, Friedemann completed the designs for this beautiful building, basing its form on the principles of sacred geometry. He then built a clay model of it, and found an architect who could work with the design and get it approved with all the county building codes and ordinances.

Friedemann was a brilliant human being. With his resources and his education he could have done anything he wanted to do in life. Because he understood the work I was doing in Eurythmy, he designed and built this building for me, and by doing so honored both me and the work of Eurythmy.

PART SEVEN

OUR DAUGHTER ENTERS OUR LIVES

Friedemann and I were soul-spiritual mates, and we had a wonderful, creative life together. But despite knowing almost from the moment we met that we deeply wanted to have a child, destiny had its own design for how that child would come to us, and we had to wait for many years. So it was that after the heartbreak of two miscarriages, Friedemann's issues with his sperm count, and my body's opening to menopause, we decided we needed to change our focus and we went to Europe.

Friedemann and I were individuals within our marriage. Even though we drank from the same bottle of wine, we drank always from two separate glasses. Typically, when we returned from Europe, I would return two or three weeks ahead of him. These short separations were a way for us to keep our marriage very alive, and also allowed our individual destinies to develop in freedom. So I came back to the US first, and a couple of weeks later I picked him up at the airport and brought him home.

The weather was perfect that afternoon, and we decided to sit in our rose garden to have tea. And that day, upon his return, we actually cried together. We had been trying to have a child for ten years and it had not happened. The yearning was so powerful that with its lack of fulfillment we actually wondered if we were meant to be separate, whether our lives and work would be more fruitful if we separated. But to that, we both said "No." We loved each other and we knew it was important that we be together for our spiritual destiny.

At that moment I said, "Who knows how she will come; maybe she'll come through adoption. "

That's all I said. We had our tea, the relationship went on, and it continued to be beautiful.

The following year, Friedemann had developed allergies, and we travelled to Portland, Oregon, for him to see a specialist who worked with natural remedies. This woman was also a friend, and that evening we had dinner with her. She mentioned that her assistant, Sarah, was pregnant and was giving her child up for adoption. She asked us if we were considering adoption and we told her we were but we had been slowed and frustrated by the whole bureaucratic process.

Some months later, I got a telephone call from Sarah. She re-introduced herself, reminded us how we had met, and then said she was going to give birth in six weeks. Then she said, "I believe this child is yours. It belongs to you."

I said, " But we understood that you had parents for this child." She replied that she had, but when she really thought about it, she felt that this child was ours. I told her Friedemann and I would discuss this and, since we were leaving for France in a couple of days, I would call her from France.

Every day Friedemann and I meditated on this child: "Is this the child? Could this be her?" One day we woke up, looked at each other, and both of us said, "Yes." We realized, this is a gift being given to us.

I called Sarah from a corner cafe way up in the mountains in France, to tell her we wanted to adopt the child. I then asked her if she knew whether the baby was a boy or a girl, and she said," It's a boy."

I said, "Are you sure? Because I keep thinking it's a girl."

She said, "No, I'm quite sure it's a boy."

I decided to buy some of the beautiful baby clothes that they make in France. I purchased soft neutral colors, because in my meditations I only saw a girl. When Friedemann and I meditated on names, no boys' names came up. We did, however, intuit a girl's name: Genevieve Vita

58

Schwarzkopf.

Shortly thereafter, we returned to California. Some weeks later, Sarah called at midnight, and told us she was going into labor. We left on the first plane in the morning. Sarah had an unusually short labor for a first child - four hours - and the baby was nine hours old by the time we got there and I was able to hold it in my arms. And it was a girl!

When I had called Sarah from France to tell her we wanted to adopt her child, I also asked her if she knew the conception date, and she did. She had not been a sexually active woman, so she was able to give me the exact date she conceived. I went back into my calendar because I wanted to know what had happened on that date. To my quiet amazement, I discovered that that was the day Friedemann and I cried having tea in the rose garden and I had said that she might come to us through adoption. Somehow our daughter's conception had resonated through to me, somehow I had known, somehow I was able to say, "She will come. Maybe it will be through adoption."

The miracle we call creation is so grand. The plan is so big and we are all actively a part of it. I believe we plan our incarnation. We even plan which parents we need in order to develop or gain certain aspects or qualities to further our individual destiny. Genevieve chose her situation very carefully, and knowing her now, I understand why. She needed us in her life for so many reasons. She needed a brilliant, compassionate father, and a mother with a background in the arts. She needed someone who loved horses, and she shared that love with her father. She needed the kind of life-guidance that I gave her as she matured. She needed the Waldorf School, extensive travel, and life adventures, all of which she had in her childhood.

I knew Genevieve quite immediately when she was still a small child. She was a miracle to me--her beauty, intelligence and openness. She also became a great teacher for me.

. . . .

When Genevieve was ten or eleven, she came home one day and asked me to take her to the Bay Area to see Amma, an Indian saint who travels to this country from India once a year. Genevieve had seen a film about Amma at a friend's house, and she knew she had to see her. So Genevieve and I drove to the Bay Area and stayed in a hotel right next to where Amma's event was being held.

Amma embraces people. Thousands of people come to these events simply to be hugged by her. People all over the world find that it is healing to be in her radiant presence.

A little shuttle bus drove back and forth from the hotel to the event hall. There were crowds of people coming and going all day long - I don't know how many thousands. Genevieve and I joined them on the shuttle bus, and went to the hall. There we saw Amma, who at that time was still a beautiful, young woman with a love power that was very healing.

After staying for a time, I suggested that we go back to the hotel. When we got there, however, Genevieve asked me if she could return by herself. Because I had friends there, and because it was so close, I agreed. She hopped on the shuttle by herself, and went back. It was even more crowded when she returned, and she stood at the back of the hall. Across this sea of people, Amma saw her. She asked her assistants to go and get that girl. The assistants approached Genevieve and brought her right up in front of everyone, and Amma blessed her.

Somehow Genevieve was recognized for who she is. During the two-day event, she received many blessings from Amma. She was taken backstage and was given personal mantras to practice, something very rarely done.

In this same month, Genevieve asked if she could stay home from school one day because four Tibetan monks were coming to our home to visit and have lunch. This child never missed school; she wanted to go to school even when she was sick. I could perceive how important this was for her, and agreed that she could stay home. She dressed herself

60

very beautifully in a sari and greeted our Tibetan guests on the front porch. After lunch the monks asked if they could work with her and took her into the library where they gave her blessings and meditations.

I felt that it was my responsibility to expose Genevieve to as many spiritual paths as I could so that she could choose freely from among many forms, if any. She experienced a Christian Community confirmation, participated in Native American ceremony, coming- of-age rituals for young women, sun dance experiences and sweat lodges. She had many initiation experiences as a young girl and was recognized by highly developed people.

As she matured, she connected most deeply with Buddhism. At one point in her high school years, when she was attending a private school in Santa Barbara, she learned that the Dalai Lama was going to speak in Pasadena, and that a close family friend, Stan Padilla, would be taking a youth group down to see him. When Genevieve's schoolmaster refused to allow her to miss one day of school so that she could travel to Pasadena with Stan to see the Dalai Lama, Genevieve quit school.

She said, "I'm not going to miss this for anything." And she didn't.

We transferred Genevieve to a school in the Bay Area. She had displayed enough of her individuality that I could trust that she would make her way.

Genevieve was a wonderful child. We had a great life. I must say that having her as my daughter was the most ideal experience I ever could have had as a mother.

Through all the years of Genevieve's childhood, I was busy all of the time -- teaching and performing eurythmy, as well as producing and directing plays. I had the energy to offer my help artistically wherever I was needed, and was in many projects. One of these, a fundraiser for Genevieve's school, was the play "The Gray Gentlemen," based on the novel "Momo" by Michael Ende. I produced and directed this play, working with a cast of students, parents, and teachers. Our performances were sold out, and we had to turn people away! It made $1200 for the school and provided a lot of fun for all of us.

Throughout this time, I also held many eurythmy classes. In 1996, a group of students asked me if I would train them in eurythmy for the next four years. I made a commitment to take this one last group of students. This formed a major part of my work during that time. These students graduated in 2000.

PART EIGHT

EXCEPTIONAL EVENTS AND PEOPLE IN MY LIFE

THE LAKOTA SUN DANCES

During all the years of our life together in California, including the time we were raising Genevieve, Friedemann and I travelled to many places, learning from people wherever we went. In 1992, I travelled to the land of the Lakota Sioux people in Pine Ridge in the season when they performed the Sun Dance. In this ancient ceremonial ritual, people dance from early morning until nightfall for four days. Some of the participants chose to have themselves pierced and hung from a tree, from morning until evening for the duration of the dances.

I returned to the Lakota people in Nebraska in 1993 to observe the Sun Dance ceremony there. Elmer Running, the medicine man normally living at Pine Ridge or Rosebud in South Dakota, gave form to this ceremony. Once again I saw piercings, although on that reservation no one was hung from the trees.

The Sun Dances are oriented in relationship to the four compass directions. Those who dance move about in a circle, and the onlookers watch them from a surrounding pavilion. At one point, the dancers grouped themselves in the shape of a "V," the way geese fly. Standing in the outer circle, I was asked to go to the West Gate, remove all my jewelry and wait. When the dancers completed the West Gate, the medicine man handed the peace pipe to me. With the subtle gesture of one of the dancers, I handed it on to the musicians, who then lit it and passed it, in a circle, to all the musicians. It was handed back to me and I was directed to smoke it, so I did.

63

When I took the pipe and inhaled, I felt the intense power of a lightning bolt of energy tear through me, just as I had felt two decades years earlier in Jerusalem. Its power left me in tears. After the ceremony concluded, someone came to collect the pipe and I stood there, still in tears. These were tears of Spirit Truth, connecting with the power of centuries of hope that one day human beings will find peace, within themselves, and with one another.

A MIRACLE WITH THE HOPI INDIANS

Friedemann and I had many different circles of friends. One close friend was Georg Kühlewind, a brilliant Hungarian chemist. He was the scientist who had invented the powder that was instrumental in quelling the devastating Kuwaiti oil field fires in 1991. More than 600 oil wells had been set ablaze by Iraqi troops as they were driven from Kuwait.

Georg was also a linguist and an author, and his research included the study of primal sounds and languages. He discovered that one of the spoken languages that contained these primal sounds was the language of the Hopi, whose villages were located on three mesas in Northeastern Arizona.

This part of the country -- the desert --had always held such a sacred meaning for me that when Georg expressed an interest in visiting the Hopi, Friedemann and I were only too happy to be his guides.

I have many vivid memories of that drive to Arizona. At one of our stops, Georg, who had packed his little camping stove and a tiny espresso maker, decided it was time for an espresso. Always the chemist, he measured out the exact amount of water and the precise amount of coffee, and then we all stood in a circle around the camp stove to block the wind from blowing out the flames. In this way, Georg was able to light the camp stove and have his espresso. Such wonderful eccentricities endeared him to me.

64

The Hopi Mesas are flat plateaus at three different levels on the tops of mountains. We planned to visit the second mesa, where the Hopi were preparing for Kachina dances to bring on the rain.

On the morning of the ceremony, we awoke to clear, blue skies. Nevertheless, we packed extra clothing and blankets into the car, in case the weather should change. When we arrived up on the mesa, we could see for hundreds of miles in all directions, and the sky was clear and blue as far as we could see.

Being a scientist, Georg said with marked skepticism, "And they are going to bring rain?"

I have seen Native Americans do remarkable things, so I responded, "We'll see." It was simple for me to believe that they could.

The ceremonial dances began shortly after we arrived at the mesa. Native American elders know how to pray. They speak to the elements through drumming, singing, and dancing, and they pray from the depths of their hearts. The Hopi have no dualism. Their spirits connect directly with the spirits of the wind, the clouds, and the rain, knowing these things are all part of who they are---of who we all are. The Native American people do not separate themselves from nature or from the elements, as we do in our modern world.

As the Hopi elders prayed for rain, things began to change. We watched the winds bring in the clouds, and felt the air grew cold and stormy. I was wearing a full-length leather coat with a hood and a thick lamb's fur lining, and was covered from the top of my head to my ankles, but I began to shiver. I wrapped a blanket around myself, but I was still cold.

Before the end of the ceremony, the rain had come. *Another miracle.*

MEETING THE DALAI LAMA

There have been many wonderful events in my life, but one of those which I actually consider to be a real miracle was my meeting with His Holiness, the Dalai Lama. This occurred at a reception in a private home in San Francisco. I was already in the home when His Holiness entered. It was announced that he had arrived, but I couldn't see where he stood, because of all the taller people in the room. Then I had the strange sensation that something like a divine force lifted me up and placed me directly in front of him.

As I stood there, I knew I was beholding a truly divine being. It seemed as though his physical body held the manifestation of Spirit totally freely, and that Spirit could manifest or de-manifest according to his will. I actually found myself standing in the area of the press with the hostess of the reception tapping me on the shoulder asking me who I was. I turned with my whole being and face shining with the emanation of his Holiness in it and she kindly allowed me to remain, with no words spoken.

After he had given his talk and blessing, he left the reception, and the rest of us adjourned to a room filled with refreshments. One of the other guests who noticed me said that I looked as though I was floating. That was exactly how I felt--no gravity.

Friedemann and I left from San Francisco for Europe the next day to attend a conference in Switzerland. I began to realize that something had changed as a result of standing in front of His Holiness. For many months I had the intense experience that all my thoughts were met with direct manifestations. As an example: I remember thinking of someone whom I hadn't seen for years, only to meet her best friend driving up to the pedestrian walk I was crossing in Switzerland a moment later.

Such things -- inner and outer -- were not separated. There was no dualism. These experiences remained at this intense level for months, and then gradually became more subtle. It gave me the measuring stick to know when I was present, truly present.

I believe that what happened with my encounter with His Holiness the Dalai Lama was that his emanation was so powerful that some of it transferred over to me and entered into me through a direct transmission. I believe this is why young people in the 1960's went to India to simply sit with their gurus, so they could experience a direct transference through energetic planes.

In the years that followed, I attended several conferences of over a thousand people at which the Dalai Lama was present. But my second direct encounter with His Holiness occurred at a "Mind and Life" conference in New York that I was invited to attend. This was a three-day gathering of about fifty scientists and Buddhists.

It was tradition that whenever the Dalai Lama left a room, people stood to show him their respect. One day, as he was leaving the room, I walked up to the door where he would be passing. He paused there to wave and say goodbye to the attendees. As he did so, he drew close and took my hand in one of his, and waved with the other. He did this twice, standing right in front of me. And I experienced a spirit being so kind and so sweet that my eyes well with tears whenever I remember that moment.

THE STATE OF THE WORLD FORUM

In 1997, Mikhail Gorbachev created the State of the World Forum, calling together leaders from all over the world to explore whether, with a combined effort, a quantum leap of consciousness could be achieved for the whole planet. Held in San Francisco, California, it created an opportunity for people who looked at life from many different perspectives to meet, including heads of state, presidents, ex-presidents, ecologists, economists, and humanitarians alike.

Friedemann was invited to attend this first Forum. When he returned home, he told me of the moment when Gorbachev and Richard Butler, the American officer who sat underground for years, at the control panel for the US nuclear warheads, walked across the stage and met. As these two men looked into one another's eyes for the first time, they both said how grateful they were that they never had to deploy nuclear weapons against each other and the world. They shook hands and then looked out and spoke to the audience. Friedemann was deeply moved to have witnessed the meeting of these two great men, extraordinary beings who had held such power that might have destroyed the planet.

The State of the World Forum was to be a one-time event, yet because it was so well received by the attendees the organizers decided to continue for several more years. Friedemann asked me to accompany him the following year.

The first evening, we heard a presentation by Tom Spencer, a keynote lecturer and the European Union's NATO representative. It was one of the most brilliant lectures we had ever heard, and both Friedemann and I were truly impressed by his extraordinary clarity of mind.

The next day, the conference discussion groups began. Because we had arrived late on the first day, we had found that most of the sessions were already filled. The one remaining open session that I was interested in attending was a discussion how NATO would relate to Russia in the light of its recently instituted policy of economic and political reform known as *perestroika*. The discussion would look particularly at how the newly democratic east bloc countries could become aligned with NATO, in the light of this policy.

The presentation was held in a long, narrow room, with tables set up in the shape of a rectangular horseshoe. At the front of the room was a table with four seats and a huge flower arrangement right in the center. These seats were for the four key presenters, who, unfortunately, would not even be able to see each other because of the flower arrangement.

There were approximately twenty-five people attending this presentations. I arrived early, in order to select a place to sit where I would be able to view the entire process. I knew very little about politics at that time in my life, and rarely watched TV or listened to the news. But now I saw that all but one of the people walking into the room were men. I had the impression that most of them were either members of the military or politicians.

At the head table, on both sides of the huge flower arrangement, sat the four representatives whom would lead the discussion. On one side of the flowers were two representatives from Russia; on the other side was the sole woman in the room, representing the United States, and Tom Spencer, whom we had heard the night before, representing not just England, but the whole of the European Union.

These four were the first to speak. And as I listened, I began to grow frustrated. My understanding of this forum and of the individual morning seminars was that it was intended to be a conversational round table, designed to not just solve the problems of the Earth but to evolve them and to provide opportunities for a collective quantum leap forward. But these four presenters were not speaking *to* one another; they couldn't even *see* each other because of the flowers on the table! As they each made their presentations, they maintained their own safe, given positions, not negotiating possibilities, not recognizing each other, not even looking at one another. What should have been—or *could* have been--a round table, in the true Arthurian sense, was instead a posturing presentation, carried out in an almost corporate, or even military mind-set. *Nothing* happened.

At the conclusion of their presentations, they said there was some time left for questions. Everyone's hand flew up, including mine. And for the first time in my life, I experienced discrimination. I was one of only two women in the room, and the others present were officers, heads of militaries, heads of NATO. People all around me were called upon to ask their questions. I was not even acknowledged. Time was running out and they said there were a few minutes left for questions. I put my hand way up - I almost stood up - and then someone said, "If there's time, you can speak."

I knew that what had just happened in that room wasn't the truth--but what could I possibly say? That it wasn't the truth?? That would not accomplish a thing. So, as the person before me was speaking, I said within myself, "Spirit, speak through me, because I don't even know what to say."

I opened my mouth and I still didn't know what words were going to flow out. This is my recollection of what I said:

"When there is a problem of any kind, we have to go to its source. If this problem is really to be solved, we cannot just bring into NATO those few nations that have separated from Russia – we have to include Russia herself. It has to be a family of nations that supports this whole organization and all of which this organization supports."

My words were articulate and exact, and they had a real impact on the people in the room. When I finished speaking, the organizers announced that the luncheon was over. To my amazement, I was immediately surrounded by members of the press, who had not been allowed to speak at the luncheon. Feeling numb, I stood there, slightly dazed, hardly remembering what I had even said. Then Tom Spencer, the British politician who represented the European Union for NATO, walked up to me and said, "I would like to speak with you. Is that a possibility?"

When I said, "Yes," he continued, "Tonight after dinner, I'll meet you at the little cafe in the Fairmont Hotel," the home of that year's forum. "Right now, however, I have to leave because I'm having an allergic reaction to something. I don't know what it is, but I have hives."

"If you would like to follow me to our room, I'll test you and give you something for the allergy," I said.

We met Friedemann on the way to the room and I introduced them. Once back in the room, I pulled out my pendulum and tested him. I told him, "It's your shirt," and gave him a remedy. He removed his shirt when he got back to his room and took the medicine. His problem was cleared immediately.

70

That evening I met with him in the Fairmont cafe. He looked at me and said, "Who are you?" This question, though seemingly simple, was very profound. At that moment, we both realized that we had something to do with one another, perhaps even a connection from another lifetime. I felt as if I had always known him. I responded to his question, "You mean *me*?" and I pointed not simply at myself but back behind and beyond myself, through time and many lifetimes.

And he said, "Yes." He knew exactly what I meant. From there we had a very profound conversation. Tom became a very fine friend, and we kept in contact over the years..

The next night the honors were given out. As conference attendees went around the room thanking presenters for their work, I came to the man who had sat underground for ten years with his finger on the nuclear button, and at the beginning of the conference had shaken hands with Gorbachev. He said, "Oh, you're the woman who was so outspoken at the NATO meeting."

I said, "Oh..."

And he said, "It was good."

This man and I began to correspond through letters, and we had very good contact over the years. I could always ask him real questions, and get real answers about the condition of the world.

I attended the State of the World Forum for three years. The last year I attended, I was commissioned to create a eurythmy performance. I invited seven eurythmists from Europe and the US to perform a powerful Shostakovich quartet with me, accompanied by the Russian Arlikan String Quartet. The performance was to be in honor of Gorbachev and the Russian delegation that year, but because of his wife's illness, Gorbachev did not attend. The performance was attended by world leaders, including many heads of state from Russia, and was most meaningful.

71

Miraculously, I had the courage to speak that first year I attended the World Forum. And that courage brought so much. The people there who had power and knowledge also had political investments. I had no investment. It is important that investments do not override truth. I had the courage to align with truth and the correct words streamed through me.

CONNECTIONS TO EGYPT

When I was in my 20's, before I moved to Europe to study eurythmy, I went through half a year of dreaming about ancient Egypt, and had some very lucid dreams. These dreams ran like a thread through my life for many, many years.

One year, the organizers of the State of the World Forum asked Friedemann to create a workshop on sustainable agriculture. In preparation, Friedemann reached out to people involved in sustainable agriculture throughout the entire world, including an Egyptian man named Ibrahim Abouleish. When he came to California to attend the State of the World Forum, Dr. Abouleish stayed with us at our home, and we got to know him well.

Today Egyptian cotton is one of the purest cottons in the world, largely because of his work. He tells how, as a young man, he had looked out over the vast desert and envisioned how he could build a thriving community there. His vision was not only to bring fertility to the earth, but also to bring vitality to the cultural life of Egypt, by building a center for the development of mankind. This would include biodynamic farming of cotton and food, as well as work, schools, hospitals, housing and more for hundreds of people.

Dr. Abouleish was born in Egypt and received his higher education in Austria, where he met his wife. When they returned to Egypt, he began purchasing fast-growing trees from New Zealand, and was able to plant whole walls of trees in the desert. These windbreaks protected the land from the biting Sahara sandstorms, and enabled vast tracts of land to be reclaimed for agriculture.

By the time Friedemann and I met him, Dr. Abouleish had developed a large living community, called Sekem, on hundreds of acres of this reclaimed desert land. There he was growing and processing biodynamic cotton, providing jobs and education for a few hundred people. He had also purchased and rented over 200 farms along the Nile and had converted them to organic/biodynamic agriculture. He worked with the Egyptian government and convinced them to stop spraying 90% of their cotton crops. He also had developed training programs for doctors, pharmacists, and educators, as well as hospitals practicing homeopathic medicine. Because of his work, one could see billboards all over Cairo offering homeopathic medicine which could help mitigate cancers in a natural way.

While he was visiting us that year in California, he also observed my eurythmy classes, and invited me to come to Egypt to teach. Over the years I visited Dr. Abouleish's SEKEM project three or four times. I was deeply impressed with this man and the vision he held of transforming the entire cotton industry in Egypt.

The last time I went to Egypt to teach, Dr. Abouleish asked me if I would help start a eurythmy school there. I was honored, but I had to tell him that I wasn't prepared to do that. I couldn't leave my life and work in California.

Also during this last trip, I met a woman who was a teacher at the SEKEM project school. Her aunt, an opera singer, was coming to visit and wanted to make a trip to the pyramids and she asked if I would like to join them. I had already visited the pyramids several times, but welcomed any opportunity to return to them. So a small group of about six of us set out with our driver for the pyramids. Traffic in Cairo was terrible, so we got to the pyramids late in the day, arriving only an hour before dusk, shortly before the pyramids would close.

Access to the pyramids is through a very small door. To reach the inner chambers, one then has to ascend through a narrow passage that slopes steeply upward, and stoop down at the top to avoid hitting one's head. At last one arrives at the inner chamber, known as the King's chamber, where the sarcophagus for the dead one rests. In ancient times, people were put into altered states of consciousness and placed in the chamber for the purpose of initiation. Light funnels into the chamber through narrow tunnels, placed precisely in such a way that the sun and certain stars would shine right on the person in the sarcophagus. Many ancient cultures understood this process of how to work with the stars, the sun, the solstices and equinoxes, in order to facilitate certain changes in consciousness in conjunction with the heavens.

Our small group climbed through the passageway, and emerged into the chamber. The stillness of the room was broken by the noise of a loud fan, used to eliminate the smell that would otherwise build up in that confined space. Because the fan was so noisy it was difficult to experience anything, I used sign language to ask the young guard to he turn it off. When he walked out of the chamber and back down the long chute to the electrical control room, I began to do eurythmy, intoning the vowels. The women in the chamber who knew eurythmy joined in a circle and moved with me. When we heard the guard coming back up, we stopped, and then the opera singer began to sing. The acoustics in the chamber were extraordinary.

When the guard returned, he gathered everyone into a circle. He took my hand and led me right into the middle of the circle, placing me above a small opening on the floor. This was clearly an energy point. He continued to stand right in front of me, and began chanting in some language that was neither Arabic nor English. I couldn't recognize it, but it was beautiful and sounded very ancient. I closed my eyes, and felt like I was lifting off the ground. It was an immensely powerful experience for me. At length, he tapped me on the shoulder and called me back to myself. When I opened my eyes, I saw that the others were all standing against the main wall of the chamber, which was also clearly an energy channel. He led me to the wall and guided me to put my forehead against it. And after some time he tapped me again. Everyone was gone. They had left the chamber. I had been guided to such a transcendent state that I did not even hear them leave.

I began walking slowly down the chute to the entry chamber. At this point everyone else had already exited the pyramid. As I emerged from the chute onto the half-way landing, there was an old gentleman dressed in beautiful silken robes. He wore a small fez-like cap. The young guard who was with me closed the chamber door behind us, because it was the end of the day. Then the old man came closer. He blessed me and kissed me on both of my cheeks. He stood and simply looked into my eyes for a moment and then we all left. I have no idea where he came from or who he was. He was just there, with the young guard, at the end.

I stepped out of the entry chamber into the evening air and stood there looking out at the Sahara and all the pyramids rising up out of the desert. It was as if I was in a dream. Everyone I had come with was already down by the car waiting for me so I climbed down and we all piled into the car. They wanted to go to the bazaar, and I went along, but I knew I was in no condition to shop. Instead, I found a little cafe, ordered an Arabic coffee, and simply sat there reflecting on what I had just experienced in the pyramid.

That was the last time I was in Egypt.

The temptation to accept Dr. Abouleish's invitation was huge. I was being offered something that was connected to an ancient past for me, just as my connection with the Native America people years before had been. I knew that if accepted, I would be well- provided for. Dr. Abouleish even offered to build me a house. But I believed my destiny was in the United States, and ultimately, I said no.

And that always means saying yes to something else!

PART NINE

ENDINGS AND NEW BEGINNINGS

Among his many areas of expertise, Friedemann had a degree in law. In 2001 he became involved in a project dedicated to environmental sustainability, and started working with a client on a patent to support the development of wind turbines in Russia. One day, he travelled to San Francisco to meet with a European patent agent to discuss the project. On his way there, he became unsure of which off-ramp to take to exit the freeway. He pulled off onto the shoulder to telephone the man he was to meet and ask for directions. Before the call had even gone through, a truck going 70 miles per hour crashed into him from behind. The driver of the truck had fallen asleep behind the wheel. Friedemann's head was slammed into the headrest. When the ambulance arrived, he was rushed to Stanford Medical Center.

It was midday when I got the call. I made arrangements for our daughter Genevieve to be taken care of, dropped everything else, and drove immediately to Palo Alto.

Stanford is considered to be one of the most advanced hospitals, possibly in the world. From a diagnostic standpoint, I think this is true. Yet as I witnessed different aspects of Friedemann's treatment, I quickly decided to move him to Auburn Faith Hospital, a local hospital closer to our home.

Friedemann's brief stay at Stanford allowed me to again reflect on the vast differences between this country's notions about medicine and healing, and Europe's. I know of clinics in Switzerland that keep lists of the contact information of alternative or complementary healers posted on the wall in the burn unit, so they can be called when a patient with urgent needs arrives. The doctors know that for certain things their work has limitations, and they make this list of alternative healers available to patients. And miraculous things happen, even over the phone, because these healers are working with physics, with energies where time and space do not have the meaning we normally attach to them. There are many, many ways to do things. The conventional form of medical practice in our country's prestigious institutions is unnecessarily limited. If it could only be practiced in conjunction with other healing forms, the results for everyone could be extraordinary.

Friedemann was paralyzed. He could not walk, he couldn't speak at all, he could barely swallow, and he certainly was unable to write. Tragically, this brilliant scholar had no outward form of expression accessible to him. He was now faced with a new life question: How do we make conscious that which is given to us naturally? How do we metamorphose those things, and in that process of metamorphosis create a living force?

Friedemann's healing process was a long and arduous one. With Friedemann closer to home, I worked at that time to gather a team of people to work with him. It was at this time that I re-met George Seeley. Thirty years earlier, our families had been friends, sharing holiday celebrations and family friendships. The George I met in 2001 was a different man. Separated from his wife, he had lived off and on in Mexico for a time, but had now returned to California. George was a skilled physical therapist, and as soon as Friedemann was ready for treatment, he became one of five therapists and healers who worked intensely with him.

By the end of a year of hard work, Friedemann could walk again, although he needed to support himself by using a cane. It was a huge accomplishment when he learned to swallow again! He was at last able to eat, and could even speak again, even though it was still a bit slurred.

In 2003, Friedemann decided he wanted to go to Northern Germany to work with a woman whom he and our daughter Genevieve had been visiting every summer. She worked with horses, and had developed a special kind of riding therapy that would be able to assist him to regain the faculty of speech. She focused on the effects that riding can have on the sacrum, whereby through the loosening the lower carriage of the body a neurological connection is reestablished that affects the speech centers in the brain.

Friedemann spent some time with this therapist, and then went to the Canary Islands when the weather turned cold. Shortly after his arrival there, he began to hemorrhage severely. He was immediately rushed to a hospital in Germany and underwent an emergency surgery. The doctors discovered a widespread cancer in his lower body, and although they removed as much of the diseased tissue as they could, they did not expect him to live more than a year.

I flew to Europe to be with him as soon as I heard what had happened. Soon, however, I needed to return to California to settle some things at home. My plans were to return as soon as possible to stay with him. When the time came to say goodbye, however, Friedemann and I looked deeply at one another, and his Spirit and mine communicated. Somehow we both knew that the end was near, even though the doctors had given him more time. We hugged, we kissed, and then we said simply, "Auf wiedersehen" -- I'll see you in the next life. There were no tears. That was our parting.

I flew back to California, and received a call only a few days later from his sister telling me he had died. It was June 10, 2003.

I didn't return to Germany. Instead, I had a memorial service in California for Friedemann. There were several speakers, among them a Christian priest, a Zen Buddhist priest, an African-American priest, and a highly-respected physicist. Over 200 people, friends and family, came together to celebrate the life of this very wonderful human being.

. . . .

After Friedemanns's death, one more chapter of my life closed. My eurythmy students had graduated in the year 2000, and the training had come to its end. I had stopped much of my performing during the time I devoted to Friedemann, until he passed.

It was then that George truly entered my life, starting another whole new chapter.

I had not thought that love could happen for me again. I was deeply in love with Friedemann on a profound level, and he was my spiritual partner. George, however, became my earthly partner, and I fell in love like a teenager.

I truly needed this at that time in my life -- someone who could help me here on this earth. And George was perfect -- beautiful, big-hearted, strong and handsome. He helped me with Genevieve, and helped me become physically active again.

In time, George and I began attending workshops together, something I had not done for many years. I had often received two or three flyers a week advertising big conferences and consciousness workshops taking place across the country, but I had put them aside without really considering them. One day, however, I saw a flyer for an upcoming workshop in New Mexico and said to George, "Let's do that. It sounds really fantastic."

One of the conference keynote speakers was a man named Alberto Villoldo. He wanted to work with members of the audience to demonstrate that human beings' chakras are powerful sources of health when they are developed, and actually a detriment if they are not. He stated that if people don't know themselves on this level of energy, other people can weaken them, whether by their thoughts or their actions. That morning he worked onstage with volunteers from the audience, and I saw that something powerful and quite exceptional was happening. I didn't know what he was doing, but I wanted to know more about it.

Such moments of awareness and heightened interest have happened at other times in my life, and they have always been turning points. Meeting Edith Gutterson in Los Angeles was one of those moments. I remember thinking, "I don't know what it is, but I can see she definitely knows something by the light in her eyes." With Alberto, through his whole gestalt, his whole being-ness, and the absolutely subtle thing that he was doing, I experienced a completely different level of energy work. His work is energetic medicine.

I made a decision in that moment to study with him. He signed a book for me that I took home and quickly read. I then signed up for his courses and began.

Years before, when Friedemann was still alive, I had begun studying a practice called "Holotropic Breath Work" with a man named Stanislav Grof. Decades earlier, he had been involved in work similar to that which Dr. Chandler in LA and Alfred and Leary at Harvard were doing. Grof and his wife then developed this breath work as a practice that took people to the threshold of consciousness and across it, facilitating a transcendent experience. They assisted people in dealing with all sorts of things hidden in their souls that led to different kinds of neuroses, and their process was phenomenal. Although I had participated in the training all the way to graduation, I never completed the course because of Friedemann's accident and death.

Now, however, I met Alberto Villoldo and my path took me even further. Alberto is a classically trained medical anthropologist. He was a faculty member at San Francisco State University, where he created a department to study psycho-somatic illness and healing. In order to investigate the effects of energy healing on blood and brain chemistry, he founded and directed the Biological Self-Regulation Laboratory.

Alberto also pursued his own personal training in shamanistic medicine, which included studies with master teachers who live in the remote mountains of Peru. As his own understanding evolved, he grew to understand how ancient wisdom and contemporary techniques can complement and illumine one another to create profound levels of healing.

For me, studying energy medicine with Alberto advanced all the healing methods and processes I had already learned. It was a wonderful training. With his work, one does not need to identify psychologically with a so-called problem. Because the work is on an energetic level, there is really no need to identify with what is "going on," with a "story." A person remains in much more of a witnessing state, which makes the transformation process very beautiful and transparent.

Life has been very generous to me. I have done so many studies and have been given so many powerful healing tools to work with. All my studies have culminated in Alberto's work. In the last few years I have taken many people through the energetic process I learned through working with him. I've worked with people with cancers so advanced that our work was really more of a preparation for death. Through my work with shamanism, I have learned to take people through threshold experiences and help them transform through to the next stages of their life work.

To complete my course work, I needed to conduct ten patient case studies. In one of my first cases, I worked with a woman who had a lot of fear. She was afraid she would develop cancer like her mother had, and die young. She agreed to let me work with her.

We crossed thresholds together, and she went right to the fear. She remembered being a little child and sitting in an underground cellar after the air raids had gone off during World War II. There she experienced tremendous fear. People were not allowed to have any light in the cellars, and everything was cold and very dark. This fear had been driven right into the core of her being.

In our work together, I took her through the process of clearing the Luminous Field until that child sitting there in that cellar was filled with light and could stand up and walk out of that cellar and that darkness. The fear was gone after that, and it never come back.

This is but one of many, many cases.

PART TEN

EXPERIENCES WITH ILLNESS, HEALINGS AND DEATH

I have touched and been touched by very many lives through my work. I have helped many people, and I have been given insights and help by many individuals on my way. I have learned how important our human relationships are for our growth.

I have also learned that whether or not we are able to move forward in our evolutionary process is only a question of whether, or when, we are able to open ourselves to new possibilities. We need to learn to *find the appropriate questions* that will enable us to take our next step. Nothing can begin until we find the question. Only thus can we become truly human.

This can become particularly evident when a person becomes ill. If a person who is ill can find their own, deep question, they will be able to access the guiding forces that live in the core of their own being. These will lead them to the people and situations they need to meet. If we can access these levels of our being, we become our own healers, we become our own priests, we become our own teachers.

People don't generally realize how much healing power there is in the world. We have to wake up to our own possibilities and potentials and believe in ourselves. We have to *trust* who we truly are. And this is the difficulty: no one actually believes that they *know*. No one believes that they can make the change in themselves, that they can actually heal themselves.

Physical medicine is a necessary help if an illness has manifested in the physical body. A disease that is affecting the body needs to be treated in the body, but that alone is not enough for true healing. If the cause of an illness is not recognized and cleared, it will repeat itself somewhere else in the body, because it did not have its original manifestation in the body.

83

The work of Alberto Villoldo focuses on clearing the "Luminous Energy Field," the more sensitive body that surrounds and envelopes the physical body. (This is also known as the Etheric Body). Everything we go through in life is imprinted in the luminous field. If something unhealthy is imprinted, it may become a cause of disease. If it is not cleared from the luminous field, it will become a physical manifestation. Conversely, if the disease is cleared from the luminous body, it will not have to manifest physically. If it does become a physical illness, then it has to be treated medically, of course, and everything is harder to treat if it manifests in the physical body. Even in that case, however, it has to be treated within the luminous body or it will have no other course but to repeat itself. Through Alberto's work, true healing can occur in the Luminous Energy Field, while getting rid of disempowering stories from the past. This life-changing work paves the way for rebirth.

A disease such as cancer is so difficult because although a person may get rid of it, it will come back sooner or later if it is only treated on the physical level. This happens if the person hasn't gotten to the source of what created the disease in the first place. Yes, it is true that there are a lot of carcinogens in our degraded environment, but cancer is not entirely a physical thing. All of us have cancer cells in our bodies, that are sometimes active and sometime inactive! Rudolf Steiner said, "It is the poor fellow who happens to go to the doctor on a day when one of these cancer cells is active. It might be only a few days later that the cell is not active."

Cancer cells are not the issue. The real question is to determine what, and when, and why any of these things become active in us. When a person's immune system is strong enough, it can eliminate even cancer cells.

. . . .

When Friedemann and I came back to California after our honeymoon trip around the world, I began to teach eurythmy and do performances in many places. One of the things that I chose to do was to offer eurythmy classes once a week at a home for handicapped children in Fair

Oaks, California. Many of the children with whom I worked couldn't walk or talk. I had to develop a way of reaching them with the elements of eurythmy. I would move their limbs and make sounds, and I would put on small presentations of little poems for them. Over time I began to sense that these children were some of my greatest teachers. They themselves couldn't speak, couldn't express anything at all beyond yelling or crying. Yet when I was "in truth" with them, something incredible would happen in their faces. Even the sounds they made became different. These children gave me a sure guide whereby I could perceive whether I was acting in truth or not. When I was not really quite there, when I was working through my ego and not through the presence of spirit, nothing happened. The fact that we were together doing eurythmy with each other was of no consequence.

There was one child, Amy, who had a habit of constantly banging her head. She was about eight years old, with a very heavy body, seemingly all gravity. Amy was catatonic; her head leaned back as far as it could, and her eyes stared blankly up at the ceiling. She never responded to anything, and it seemed as if no one was home at all. My co-workers believed that Amy was so far away from her body that she didn't even know what was happening or understood what anyone said, and they didn't hesitate to speak freely around her. They were pretty conscious people and spoke decently, but they really believed she didn't understand anything.

One day I went to work and saw Amy sitting in her little wooden chair, banging her head extremely hard against the back of her chair. I couldn't believe what I was seeing! She was hitting her head so hard she could have beaten herself into a concussion. I got down on my knees in front of her, and I felt something pouring into me, a passion in me about this being, this little girl's life.

I said to her very directly, "Amy, this is not the truth."

And she stopped. She pulled her head back around and stared me right in my eyes and then I knew that she understood everything. It was like a key. I had found the key. With all children of that nature there is a key, and if your intentionality is strong enough and you have determination, you will find that key.

From that day on, all I had to do was walk in the front door of that home and no matter where Amy was in the building, she would acknowledge my presence with happiness. They said she always knew the exact moment I entered the home. The only way I can explain it is that I had connected to her on an energetic plane. I had spoken to her true being and she responded.

Much later, I read Amy's medical records. When she was a very little girl, her grandparents were murdered in Sacramento. At that precise same moment, Amy had an epileptic seizure in her home on the other side of Sacramento. We are all so open and delicate -- we truly experience *everything*. Most of us don't know that the reason we experience everything is because we have points in our consciousness that close doors to protect us. Amy didn't have these doors. She experienced her grandparents' death directly and went into an epileptic seizure and had these fits from then on. From there, she slipped into a catatonic state where she no longer entered her body. It was too painful on the earth for her.

Some time in the spring, I told the children the story of Easter. I was working with the children individually and I began with Amy. I began telling her about Easter and then I told her how much we needed her here on the earth -- how much we need all people to help other human beings. I explained that we are all brothers and sisters.

Then I thought to myself, "I wonder if she even hears what I am saying or is this just my wishful nature? Here's a child who can't speak, has no outer reflection whatsoever about anything. And here I am, telling her my thoughts about Easter, about this love -- the essence of loving one another and helping one another...."

But I then spoke to her and said, "Amy, if you understand what I am saying to you, please find a way to lift your arm and put your hand in my hand."

86

This child had no use of her limbs, none. She was non-responsive. She had to be fed, she had to be carried. But I could feel, in the core of my being, in the core of my heart, that she understood what I was saying.

And I said, "Amy, I know you understand me and what I'm saying to you," and I proceeded to speak to her and instruct her thinking to allow her to generate the correct thought forms and light forces through her limbs, activating the life force. I guided her consciousness from the brain to the hand.

I waited. For a long time nothing happened. And then, Amy lifted her arm and put her hand in my hand.

These are the things we call miracles. Born out of absolute love for the other. Born out of belief in them and belief in a core principle of humanness -- that beyond anything, even beyond anything we call a handicap, something else can happen.

I have had miracles occur in my life, and my connection with Amy was one of them. Sadly, her parents later had to place her in a conventional care home for handicapped children where there were not personal insights into her individuality. When I visited her there, I had the impression that she had once again left her body and was no longer present.

. . . .

In 1990, Friedemann and I were preparing for a trip we had planned to Sweden. Genevieve was four at the time, and I was packing, for we were scheduled to leave the next day.

Suddenly I was doubled over with excruciating cramps. The pain was agonizing. Thinking it was the stomach flu, I called a homeopathic doctor who stopped by the house on his way home. "This is serious," he said. "You should go to the hospital and have a sonogram."

We postponed our trip, so I could get an examination. My doctor told me, "What I see on the sonogram looks dangerous. I want a gynecologist to check it." The following Monday, a gynecologist read a second sonogram, and told me I had a five-centimeter tumor that was hemorrhaging internally. My belly was painfully distended. I was urged to have an immediate operation.

My intuition told me to do otherwise. I told him, "No. I don't believe that is the way to go."

I then asked him, "Could the tumor kill me?"

"Maybe it wouldn't not kill you, but it is very dangerous and very painful. And I certainly do not recommend that you fly to Europe. Your blood thins at those altitudes and you could take yourself out that way."

I thought about it. I asked my homeopathic doctor to give me something to stop the hemorrhaging and we re-booked our flight. We travelled to Järna, Sweden, which is a beautiful place set on a fjord with a biodynamic farm and a dairy. I was still bloated and in a lot of pain, so I checked in to an Anthroposophical clinic there. Because the tests showed that I had a severe infection, I agreed to have a biopsy some days later in nearby Stockholm. The day before I was to travel to Stockholm, I had a dream. A petrified asp was lying on the ground. I picked it up and it came to life and bit me. I looked at my arm and I could see the snake's venom moving through my veins. I could sense the danger of it traveling to my heart.

In that dream moment, I looked out across the landscape and I saw a pharmacy. As I began walking toward it, a very loud voice said, "Heal thyself." I woke up with these words resounding in my mind.

Some moments later, the nurse came in with the morning medications, and I said to her, "Cancel the biopsy. I'm checking out of the clinic tomorrow." Soon the doctor came in. I have always found that Swedes are some of the mildest people on the planet, and this man was no exception. But when he heard my decision, he became outraged.

In his frustration, he began to raise his voice. "You were committed to having the biopsy, and now you are not doing it! This is critical! You really need to have this done!!"

He went on and on for quite awhile, and I waited for him to stop. At last I could say, "Look, this is my body. I manifested this tumor, and I will de-manifest it. I will leave tomorrow."

He looked at me and said, "As your doctor, I have to advise you to have this biopsy. As a human being, I admire your fight."
He gave me a powder to manage the hemorrhaging, in case I should need it, and told me to stay in Sweden for some weeks in case anything severe happened. I thanked him for his support and went to stay at my friend's home in Köchenberg, Sweden, for some days.

Friedemann and I had been scheduled many months in advance to teach in Budapest, Hungary the next week. I knew I would only be able to manage to give two or three classes during the week, although I was scheduled to teach every day. We went on to Budapest to honor our teaching commitment.

While there, in Budapest, I read a book by Stylianos Atteshlis (Daskalos), who was known to be a great healer from Cyprus. This book affected me deeply. Because of it, I began to meditate differently, and at a very deep level. This opened for me another part of my being that knew it could heal the tumor in my body. I worked very intensely on it every day, with visualizations.

I now understood how human consciousness, when directed with full attention and intentional force into any one place, acts like a laser beam of power. It is able to direct energy. This is, in fact, exactly what the Navajos worked with.

Because I had been so profoundly influenced by Daskalos' book, Friedemann suggested that we go to Cyprus, where he lived, so that I could meet him. When we got there, Daskalos examined all three of us. He worked with Friedemann's acoustic tumor, as well as with

Genevieve, who was pigeon-toed. He told us, "Don't let them operate on her. As she gets older, her weight will balance things out." (Which it did.)

Then he asked me why I was there. I explained about the tumor but I said it was gone. He asked how I knew it was gone and I said, "I know it is." He looked over me as though I were transparent. I could feel him looking right through my body, right into it. He said, "Yes. It has gone."

When we returned to California six weeks later, I thought I should go to my gynecologist.

Before I had left for Europe he had said, "Jeane, I know you can do remarkable things, but this is very serious."

When I told him there was no other way for me he said, "If you can do this, I will be a believer!" Nonetheless, on my way to his office I felt anxiety, which is a very rare thing for me. Was it possible that I had tricked myself? Could the tumor still be there?? I felt like a Doubting Thomas. I went into the reception room. The nurse greeted me and said the doctor had just left on an emergency delivery. I laughed at myself and my doubter all the way home, for I recognized now at a core level that that was just my test, and that everything was okay.

However, I still made another appointment with my doctor, and this time he spent thirty minutes under the examination drape, poking around, looking around, doing sonograms. He kept coming up saying, "I can't find anything!"

And then he would go back down. He finally straightened up, put his tools away, and said, "It's a Miracle!! What did you do? It's gone!!!"

I said to him, "OK, this is what I did," and I explained my process.

In the end he said, "Only you could have done that, Jeane." I replied, "No. What I did is available to every single human being. It's all there. Even a little bit of doubt can undermine and block the

90

movement and flow, but if the attentional consciousness can be totally harnessed and directed, our endless human capacity is all there, waiting for us to use it."

....

When Genevieve was still an infant, Friedemann started having severe headaches. He had MRI's done and was diagnosed with an acoustic tumor behind his ear which was not only growing but, because of its proximity to major nerves, was likely to be inoperable. There was no way a surgeon could get to the tumor without having to cut through nerves that controlled one side of his body.

I said, "There has to be an alternative to this."

We started our search for alternatives, looking for the great healers living on the earth. We were directed to a Native American medicine man, a Lakota Sioux. In the middle of winter, Friedemann travelled to the Pine Ridge Indian Reservation in South Dakota to meet Elmer Running. He went through days of healing ceremonies, and when he returned home something had clearly shifted. He felt better.

Soon afterwards, a friend of Friedemann told him about a healer in Europe who might be able to help him. This man, a former engineer, had invented an apparatus that could read a person's energetic pulses as they reacted to the power of specific words. He had hundreds of little cards with words written on them. He would place these cards, one by one, on a person's solar plexus, and then test the individual's energetic reaction through kinesiology. Based on each person's specific patterns, he placed selected cards into a machine, which then organized a vibrational frequency and imprinted it onto a saline water solution. This solution could bring light back into the cells of the body which had been diminished or deadened. Clearly this man was working with things that are light years away from our western medical model's understanding. Friedemann spent some time working with this man and receiving these medicines, and noticed a change almost immediately.

91

When he returned from Europe, Friedemann started to do long intensive meditative work - sometimes for three or four hours. He had incredible breakthroughs with this meditative life. He was able to make quantum leaps and shifted his consciousness. Through his inner work, he was able to stop the tumor from growing any larger. It was no longer active.

Between his meditative work, the medicines he received, and the healing ceremonies conducted by the Lakota Sioux medicine man, Friedemann's condition began to stabilize. The tumor was still present, but it had stopped growing. (This was confirmed for us through an MRI done 15 years later, at the time of his car accident.) His walking was slower and not as steady as it had been, but that did not stop him. He wrote his Ph.D. dissertation and received his doctorate with the highest honors possible. His whole life was launched in a different direction. Our life continued on. We lived a good life for twenty-one years of marriage.

. . . .

In the year 2000, my youngest sister Jeri was extremely ill. My older sister Terry, who lived near her, called me and said, "Jeri is dying. The doctors have done extensive tests, including bone marrow tests, and they can't find what's wrong with her. She can't move. She can't even turn over in bed. She's very thin and she's just lying there, waiting to die. What can you do, Jeane? Who do you know who can help?"

I hung up the phone and immediately contacted the doctor in Europe who had helped Friedemann with his acoustic tumor. He told me to send him a photograph of my sister. My brother-in-law took the photo that day and sent it by email. Within four days, my sister had a full diagnosis and a medicine that the doctor express-mailed from Europe. He had discerned a vicious virus under her left lung. I then learned that my sister had complained of a severe pain in that part of her chest, but no one had been able to discover the cause. Working with vibrational medicine, this healer from Europe was able to heal my sister in only two weeks from a painful condition which had gone undetected by her

92

western doctor, and which could have killed her.

....

Sometimes we meet people who are on the threshold of death.

In the early 1980's I was living with Friedemann in Peaceful Valley, California. Dr. Knauer wanted to move to the area and had asked me to find a home for him to rent. Then one day, his wife called me and said, "Jeane, Doctor is in Palo Alto and has had a severe stroke while visiting his daughter. If you want to see him, you need to come soon."

I drove to the hospital and found a crowd of people outside his room, and I thought that meant he had died. His wife, however, greeted me and said, "No: his bed linens are just being changed." I asked if I could go in.

He was barely alive. He was stooped and crooked in the chair as they changed his bed. I sat in front of him and called softly, "Doctor....Doctor......Doctor Knauer...." for a long time before he made any response. Then slowly, as if from a long distance, he said, "...oh.....Jeane...". It was striking to hear his voice: it was very objective, as if his spirit was using it from another dimension.

I said, "Half of your body is warm, with life force, half is cold."

And he replied, "I am on the other side, but my body has not let go."

In that moment, I said, "Have you ever allowed anyone to ever help you in the ways you have helped others?"

With hesitation, he slowly answered, "No."

"This is perhaps why you need to stay," I said. There was a long pause.

Then he opened his eyes, and spoke. He returned, and his family was astounded. Dr. Knauer had found a reason to return to this earth: to allow others to help him, and to learn to accept help.

Dr. Knauer lived many years after that. I could see that sometimes there are important lessons to be learned at the threshold of life and death. If a person has not fulfilled their destiny when they come to that threshold, they may choose to remain on earth, as he did.

....

When we die, or when we pass through what is called Death, a person's physical body returns to the physical earth. The etheric, or life body, which is connected directly to the physical organization as long as we are alive, separates from the physical body and returns to the All. This process of separation takes approximately three days. It is possible to watch this happen by observing how the color of the dead person's skin gradually fades in the course of these three days, beginning at the feet and moving up to the hands and face. As long as there is color in the body, that being is still present.

Edith Gutterson was the first person I saw dead. This occurred when I was still a young woman living in Hollywood. I was asked to sit with her body from 11 p.m. to 1 a.m. to meditate and pray with her. At 85 years old, Edith was the oldest friend I had, and I was honored to sit with her. I went by myself. Her body lay in its coffin in the chapel, in preparation for the funeral service that would be held the next day.

I walked into the chapel. There were soft lights and candles surrounding her coffin. As I approached it, it was a shock to see her lifeless body. I sat down in a chair beside her, and began reading silently from one of her favorite books, The Gospel of St. John.

Suddenly, at the midnight hour, all the lights went out. The shock of sitting with her with only the flickering candles created such a kundalini rush of energy streaming up my spine that I felt paralyzed. Every fear I had ever had of death rushed through me. After a long while, I noticed floor lamps that I could turn on. But because I still had fear pulsing through me, I decided to sit there in the dark and simply work through the fear.

I know Edith helped me with this. She was a spiritual guide to me when she was alive and she kept it up even after her death! I was supposed to be there to comfort her in her moment of death and instead she comforted me in the moment of my fear.

The day of her funeral service, I saw Dr. Knauer standing by her coffin and speaking to her. I observed how he spoke to her knowing she was still present.

Death has become a great teacher for me, and it is not what we have come to believe in our western culture.

. . . .

Soon after I arrived in Dornach to start my training in Eurythmy, I took a job at the Ita Wegman Klinik, working as a nurses' aide. On my first day at the clinic, I was told that Lori Meyer Smits, had just died, She was the eurythmist who had received the very first lessons in Eurythmy by Rudolf Steiner himself in 1912. Her body had been placed in the chapel there at the clinic. The small space was candle-lit, filled with flowers, and peaceful. In those three days, I went to the chapel in the morning, left to go to work, and then returned to the chapel later in the day. I observed the process of change in her body, just as I had with Edith. I saw how this process started at the hands and feet and moved up the limbs.

For me the color was a sign that the being was still connected to the body and should not be disturbed. This belief was later confirmed by studies I did in Tibetan Buddhism that directs that the corpse should not be disturbed after "death" until the soul has released from the physical body. The soul of the being is still present as long as color remains in the skin.

The Ita Wegman Klinik had a practice of hosting a three-day vigil for people who died. Observing this three-day process helped me overcome the dualistic conception of life and death.

95

In the early hours of the morning, one day in 1982, I received a frantic phone call. In her sweet Swiss accent, a dear friend, Veronica Moyer said, "Jeane, Jeane, it's Willi! I think he's dead!"

I said, "What do you mean, you think he's dead?? He's either dead, or he's not!"

And she said, "Then he's dead. Come immediately!"

I lived only five minutes away, and when I arrived at their home, I found him lying in his bed, his arms crossed like a pharaoh's. He had been dead for perhaps five hours. His ears were blue, and his color was already ashen. Because he had worked with Astrosophy (star wisdom) for so many years, he knew how to take leave of his body quickly, and his transition appeared seamless.

Most people in the Christian-oriented west take about three days to separate from their bodies. By contrast, in the Tibetan tradition, a high lama at the time of his death is placed in a sitting position with the legs crossed, facing east. It is possible for some to continue to stay near the body in for weeks, and people care for him until they know he has left the body completely.

....

I have helped many people pass through the gate of death. I have simply stood there with them and offered light forces through meditation to help them find their way. But people in the western world fear the great threshold called death. Everyone is terrified of it because our concepts and ideas are so intellectually hardened, and frozen in fear. We are really imprisoned in these dead, limiting thoughts that don't allow us to know life and death as a continuum. In truth, everything simply IS. All of life is a continuum.

I myself have had two encounters with death. The first occurred when I was a child of 12 years old, playing in the ocean. Suddenly a powerful rip tide pulled me away from the shore. I remember looking down, down, down into the bottom of the sea. Then I went unconscious. I felt totally peaceful with the process and had no fear. It was only when I woke up on the beach with a crowd of people around me that I realized I had almost drowned.

The second encounter occurred when I was in my forties, visiting the ancient city of Cusco, in the Peruvian Andes. There I suffered from altitude sickness, and one morning I became so ill that I passed out of my body. I lay in my bed, but I could not move, and although I could see Friedemann, I couldn't speak. As I lay there, all the life-bearing fluids of my body began flowing out of my eyes, nose and mouth. My etheric body was separating from the physical. My entire life passed before me, allowing me to resolve all karmic debts and forgive all those who had hurt me and ask for forgiveness.

Friedemann went down to the lobby of the hotel and asked for a doctor. They immediately sent someone with an oxygen tank to rescue me, but not before I saw the GREAT LIGHT, that many before me have spoken about. I was passing through the threshold of death. Just before I left, however, people put an oxygen mask on me and brought me back into consciousness.

Upon reflection, I realized that both in the case of the drowning and in the case of altitude-oxygen deprivation, I was experiencing death through a kind of suffocation.

From Cusco, we traveled on to Machu Pichu, where I had many powerful experiences. These gave me insight into *why* I had to almost die. Coming that close to death allowed me to come much closer to life, because I could witness how close the two Worlds really are!

97

PART ELEVEN

LIVING WITH TRUST

When you're in your twenties, you may not realize that you are young and your thinking may not be entirely accurate, but nevertheless, you do the best you can. What I have seen and learned is that some of the things that came to me in my twenties have proven themselves over the many years of my life. And now I am 77 years old.

We are all individuals, plucked, in a way, out of a great wholeness of spirit. All human beings are totally and absolutely whole, equipped with everything they need to unfold the true essence of who they are. But in the individualizing process we forget what and who we really *are*. We forget the essence, the source.

I believe that deep inside every human being is this *"knowing."* But what is it that allows one human being to grasp that knowing and not another? What is revealed when we explore certain destiny patterns, karma, carry-over from one lifetime to the next? Older souls? Younger souls? What is the seed that determines a life?

I believe that we create circumstances in our lives so that we can meet situations and clear karmic patterns which may have been with us for many lifetimes. Even the most difficult, painful situations can be viewed for what they are: opportunities to meet and clear karma. Looked at in this way, we are our own creators; we create our destinies.

If we can truly take full responsibility for our lives, if we can accept that no matter what happens to us, be it dreadful or wonderful, that which occurs is our own projection. We have created it. Through the cleansing and transformation of our etheric and astral bodies (or, as Alberto Villoldo refers to it, our "luminous field"), we have the possibility of creating a new future, of *dreaming our world into being.*

It is completely possible for us to move past all our self-doubting and begin to trust and have gratitude for all the moments in our lives which give us these opportunities to transform ourselves. The absolute perfection of the divine is far beyond what we can grasp. It is so vast that even if we touch only a tiny bit, even if we get the smallest glimpse, this can give us the courage and incentive to want to *know*.

Here, however, is a real problem. If people don't want to know, if they don't want to uncover things and discover a greater truth in themselves, it will not come into being of its own. It may require a very big shock. Many people have accidents or illnesses in order to wake up! And even then, some people in those situations really wake up to something glorious, whereas others simply can't reach out past themselves for the "golden ring" of wakefulness. These then are the ones who truly suffer. The devastation of spiritual stagnation that sets in after a lost opportunity can stay with them and create illness, can stay with them until they die.

What I have learned is that it is possible to live in a condition of absolute trust. I remember one morning when I was in my early twenties. I awoke to the realization that I had absolutely no money. I didn't know how I was going to pay my rent, or even eat. I didn't even have any change. I had absolutely nothing.

And this is what happens to people. They wait until they reach this absolute nothing--and then what? Usually, when this happens, panic sets in. People begin a steady stream of panic in their minds: "O my god, I can't pay the rent, I have no food, I have no money, how am I going to make it???" Then there are others who realize that moments like this are golden moments, challenges we create for ourselves. My health challenge with the tumor was one of those golden moments. It came to me in order for me to overcome it, to realize myself as the healer. Because we are the only healers; doctors can offer help, but we must heal ourselves.

And so that morning in my twenties, when I realized I had no money, I didn't panic. Instead, I reached for a little book I had and opened it randomly, because I knew that if I could do that in truth, I would have the answer. I realized in that moment that fear is the culprit. What matters isn't about what we have or do not have. What matters has to do with our ability to heal or to work through problems with our minds clear. Fear paralyzes that ability. Because I saw that clearly, I was able to release all fear and become very calm. I went into a still meditative state.

Shortly thereafter, something hilarious happened. Within an hour, there was a knock on my door. A friend of mine in Las Vegas had just won a sum of money and sent me a money telegram!

Such a thing had never happened to me before or since, but it confirmed for me that if we see through the fear that obscures our real seeing, our problems dissolve. They go away.

I never had any money fear after that. I knew that somehow things would always work out. I would never starve. I would never be without.

. . . .

When I met Friedemann, who would become my future husband, I had no idea who he was. There was a profound quality to him, his clothing, his apartment, the car he drove. He lived simply and modestly. It wasn't until we were on our way to San Francisco to be married that he told me about his family of origin in Germany and their considerable wealth. When he told me that, I started crying. I was actually crying so hysterically he had to pull the car off the freeway.

I said, "I don't know if I want the karma that goes with that kind of money." We almost turned around, but we didn't. We drove to San Francisco, met with the priest who was to marry us, and brought this issue to him.

My whole life changed upon meeting and marrying Friedemann. Suddenly, and for the first time, I had more money than I needed, more money than I could spend. I felt almost shy about buying things, so Friedemann would buy me clothes. He would come home with bags and bags of clothes that always fit me perfectly, knowing what would be just right for me.

In the first years of our marriage, I had to learn to deal with money. I faced a new fear that was strangely akin to the fear I had the morning I woke up fifty years ago with nothing to eat. It was the same fear, the same neurosis, just the opposite side of the coin. People are not their poverty, nor are they their money. But as my mother always said, she would rather be miserable with money than be miserable without it.

Our first big financial portfolio meeting was in Munich in 1979. Ours was an important account for that bank, so the meeting was with the head of Deutsche Bank and the six representatives who managed our account. I had told Friedemann in advance that for me to be involved with any part of that money, I did not want to have any investments that could lead to the harm of any human beings or the environment, including investments in munitions, pharmaceuticals, pesticides, and such. I went in to that meeting with Friedemann, who held a very important portfolio for this bank. What I, his wife, had to contribute was that I had worked out the mysteries of money, and learned to overcome both the fear of not having it and the fear of having it.

Friedemann expressed our decision to shift the direction of our investments away from anything promoting warfare and environmental degradation, and the head of the bank blew up. He lost his temper and started actually yelling at us. He knew that the restrictions we were placing on our investments were going to lose money and he was initially extremely rude. Over the years that followed, however, these people did work very decently with us, taking to heart our investment restrictions.

When Friedemann died, I really searched for the right portfolio managers, the right advisors. I moved the entire investment portfolio to San Francisco. Every person working with me is either a Buddhist or a yogi. These are clean, honorable, and good people. Of course, one does not make a lot of money this way, because one can only earn large returns if one invests in things I want nothing to do with. I simply do not want the karma that goes with the possible link between myself and

102

the harm that could befall someone on the other side of the world. This for me is the most important thing: that every deed I do, to the best of my awareness, works toward the betterment and the positive support of others, and never creates harm.

. . . .

There is absolutely no limit to the possibilities of human beings. This life is given to us. It is a gift to be in a human body. How we develop what we are given, and whether or not something in us wills to unfold the magic, the mystery, of this given lifetime, this is where we are free to choose. We can do that any way we want. We can do that with great honor and high spirit or we can do it with fear and greed.

"Freedom" is a word that is often misunderstood. It is nothing external; rather, it is a state of being. Freedom has much, much less to do with what is outside and much, much more to do with what is inside. It helps, of course, to have a certain amount of outer freedom in the world, but real freedom has to do with our inner life and with whether or not our thinking is free -- free from prejudice, free from judgments, free from preconceptions and all compulsion.

Prejudice and judgment are things we may have internalized in any number of ways – from our parents, our religions, our education. Often, or perhaps primarily, it may come from that which we bring with us.

Through the events of our lives, we put ourselves into situations where we can have the possibility of meeting these things and consciously transforming them.

We are all given so many opportunities for choice. Once we start lifting the veils away --whether it's the fear of money, the too much or the too little, or the illness that can attack the body, which is very vulnerable-- how do we honor that in us which really knows the truth? How do we choose to listen to that first? It is in any case certain that we will get challenged all along the way. The question is, how will we respond to the challenges?

I have gone through many difficult things in my life. Some of them were so impossible that I didn't know how I would manage to work through them, yet those were the moments in which I grew the most. In my struggle to find truth, to find the solution, I was always able to pull myself up. I trusted in that core essence in me that *knows*, and it pulled me upright, every time. I realized that it is precisely at such moments of growth and transformation that miracles happen.

For me, this growth happened when I reached a certain point of humility in my soul. I wanted so much to see a way to work with any situation that came before me, that I was willing to see the truth, no matter how difficult it might be.

Now I realize that I see small miracles all the time. I see it even in everyday events like making contact with a human being I never met before. Suddenly, there we are, in a moment, speaking together. Through our exchange, certain things are answered for them, for me. A friendship suddenly blossoms, even though we may never see each other again.

As I have grown older and my life has smoothed out, I realize that I could initiate and sustain my growing through meditation and keeping myself fit in my body. If the body is not fit, it can impede us and distract us from our deeper unfolding.

We need a clean diet, more strenuous exercise, regular meditation and peaceful contemplative time in nature. Watch the big birds fly -- especially when they catch the wind currents and they soar. When you get into difficulties, imagine yourself as the Eagle and fly, soaring at great heights, seeing into far distances. It helps put things into such a beautiful perspective.

PART TWELVE

FINAL THOUGHTS

This is something I have come to understand: the reality we live is our own creation. There was a period in my life when I found myself witnessing this every morning upon awakening. As I woke, I had the experience that I was peering through a long tunnel of ideas, and seeing, observing and thinking how we create the reality that we are living.

We make some decisions, I believe, before we incarnate, and these are a part of our unfolding destiny. At the appropriate times, we take up the threads from the past that need to be transformed in our present life.

I realize this more and more as I go through life: the physical body of the human being is a molecular structure, a field of energy. If we can "think away" our given form and recognize the underlying principle that structures and individualizes us in our present life, then we arrive at a different perception of reality.

At this stage of evolution, human beings want to find confirmation for spiritual realities, and they look for confirmation in the various religions. I think, however, that what is really occurring is that this spirit reality can only be perceived if we clothe it in familiar images. We may remember the story of how the native people on the shores of the Americas could not see the ships of Christopher Columbus approaching their land because they had no concept of "ships." Their shaman first had to describe the ships on the water, in order for the natives to be able to perceive them. They were incapable of perceiving "ships" because they had no corresponding concept.

The way that we conceive the world determines what we perceive. The person who is color-blind sees a colorless world: the person who hears harmonic patterns hears music with a richness others cannot share. What is truly miraculous here is that each human being sees and understands the world out of his or her own subjectivity. Humans thus project onto the things they perceive in accordance with their life orientation. The person who looks at the world with the eyes of a materialist will see a materialistic world: the person who looks at it with the eyes of a religious person will see the handwork of their own identified God in the world.

Thus, each person or each religion creates and projects their own expectation of God as they try to find confirmation for a spiritual reality. Indeed, the whole content of what we perceive is our own projection, for we have no other way to identify and unite with the world without this projection onto it. The poet-monk Angelus Silesius put it well: "The eye with which I see God is the same eye with which God sees me."

In our present age, we experience that we are separate from the world we live in. We live in a natural state of dualism. It will be a long time before we overcome this way of experiencing things and are able to perceive the world objectively. We must realize this seeming illusional separation as a stage of development. Great avatars don't need to go through such a process: they know spirit, unveiled.

There are no mistakes. We ourselves choose and create the experiences we have in order to have the possibility of transforming them in this lifetime. In his writings, Rudolf Steiner explains about the incredibly difficult, painful events that can happen to us. We ourselves have designed such events so that we can awaken to the spiritual realities which surround us, and with which we can meet the trial. We come into each incarnation with a clear plan to set up our own personal obstacle course, to confront the things we need to work out from present and past incarnations. When we are aware of this fact, we can find the courage we need to transform them.

Nevertheless, some situations are so complex that one cannot completely transform then in one lifetime. The Buddhists are speaking of this when they say, "Human beings are caught on a cog of the wheel of life."

Through the many experiences and events of my life, I have learned

106

that through the very act of cognition or realization, things can be transformed. This cognition can stop the otherwise innate momentum of a situation so something new can enter. Quantum leaps can happen when the mind can clearly see the phenomena and take hold of something completely with consciousness. When we investigate something with a clear consciousness, pieces come together almost of themselves and reveal what is really happening. When that happens, you become aligned to the deeper truth of phenomena. You can be involved in shifting the energetic planes, creating the possibility of a different interfacing with the world. Evolution happens.

I do not believe in duality as a necessary condition of being human or in the inevitability of remaining in such polarities. To be sure, these poles are an important part of the pendulum swing of polarization, and these dynamics still play a very powerful role in our evolution. They serve us in our search to find the true light. If we can work with them, we too can awaken to something deep within our primal being. If we lived only in the light from the moment we were born, we would have no need to come to Earth.

There have been great beings, like St. Francis, or the Buddha, who were able to overcome darkness, after passing through many trials. There are also beings known as the Bodhisattvas who have a free choice about whether or not to incarnate onto the earth. These beings live on earth as servants of humanity, taking on human form in order to help humankind and its evolution.

I deeply believe that eventually the planet will again go through a mass destruction, as it did at the end of Atlantis, and Lemuria before that. Yet I also believe that even after such destruction, it will once again strive towards a continuing human evolution, intimately tied to the earth's own evolution as a cosmic participant in the greater Universe. I believe that the core of humanness, the primal core, is oriented towards the Good. No matter what else occurs, we will eventually evolve towards this deeper and greater understanding of love. Somewhere, in the core of our being, we all know that love is the only thing that truly matters. Whether in our relationships to our selves, our partner, our neighbors, the animals around us, or the planet itself, love is the healing element. It is the ultimate form that human beings will choose to embrace .

Jeane Moore Schwarzkopf

Jeane Moore Schwarzkopf is trained in both film and stage. She has produced directed and performed the works of Shakespeare, Christopher Fry, Tennessee Williams and Greek Dramas, among others. Her first training was in dance at the age of seven when she became interested in classical and modern dance. She fulfilled her study of movement with six years of training in classical Eurythmy, derived from the ancient Greek temple dances. She holds the equivalent of a Masters Degree in the Arts from the Goetheanum, near Basel, Switzerland. She has taught and lectured and performed in many parts of the world including Russia, Finland, Hungary, France, Switzerland, the Philippines, Japan, and the USA. Presently, she lives and travels between Europe and California teaching, lecturing and performing upon request. She has also studied curative Eurythmy, a medical aspect of Eurythmy that is practiced in clinics all over Europe. In this capacity she works with handicapped children, accident victims and cancer patients. She studied 'Holotropic Breath' with Stanislav Groff and trained for four years with Dr. Alberto Villoldo, medical anthropologist, psychologist and shaman. She practices all of these healing modalities, in accordance with the need of the patient.

Made in the USA
San Bernardino, CA
07 April 2016